0825 Ferrara, Pal. Schifanoia — Marzo, Minerva trionfante, Ariete,
Borso parte per la caccia (affr. di scuola ferrar, attr. a Cossa o
al Tura, 1469) — Ediz. F. lll Alinari Firenze

Raphael, Parnassus (detail of Dante's head) Stanze di Raffaello, Vatican
Reproduced with permission of SCALA NEW YORK/FLORENCE

Dante and Pound
The Epic of Judgement

Dante and Pound
The Epic of Judgement

by James J. Wilhelm

UNIVERSITY OF MAINE PRESS

Orono, Maine

CRRRR

This book is number _____ of a

specially bound limited edition

of 100 signed by the author,

_____

CRRRR

The endpapers consist of two panels from the Room of the Months in the Schifanoia Palace of Ferrara, created by Cosimo Tura and Francesco del Cossa for the Este family. The panel on the left represents the month of April, ruled by Venus, the goddess of love, over the zodiacal sign Taurus. The right panel honors Minerva, the goddess of chastity and knowledge, and the month represented is March, the time of the Ram.

Library of Congress Catalog Card Number: 74-22708.
ISBN 0-915032-01-5

For
RUTH WILHELM SOUTHERLAND

TABLE OF CONTENTS

PREFACE

This study was undertaken because there seemed to be a clear need to explicate the many Dantesque references in the writings of Ezra Pound. To begin with, I was content to trace down and explain the borrowings in a rather encyclopedic way. As the book progressed, however, I became increasingly aware of the dramatic shift in Pound's uses of the Italian master, a shift that should become apparent from a reading of Chapters 7 to 9. Also, I noticed that an examination of Pound's sometimes eccentric handling of the medieval poet forced me to re-examine the Italian works, and frequently I emerged with a new and fresh viewpoint toward these things that I would not have guessed possible. I doubt that any seasoned Dantista will learn much from Pound or this book, but certainly the general reader may see the Italian in a more vigorous perspective.

At the outstart, I would like to establish some guidelines. Pound is, as everyone knows, often difficult and sometimes inconsistent. Therefore, in quoting him, I have allowed his words to stand intact, making *sic* comments only for a few of the more obvious English misspellings. One thing must be borne in mind: Pound used the 1921 Società Dantesca text for most of his Dante citations. I use more recent editions of the *Comedy* and other works. As a result, our citations often do not correspond exactly, although the differences are minor. I italicize all of my own citations from Dante's Italian and use quotation marks on my own English translations inside the text. Unless Pound or someone else is clearly named as the translator, the work is mine.

In the first six chapters of the book, I employ footnotes, but I have dispensed with documentation during the three analytical chapters, where the text is already dense with interior citations. I include a Select Bibliography to direct the reader to the most recent and useful Dante and Pound criticism in book form. After Donald Gallup's brilliant bibliographic study, any short compendium of Pound's work must seem a mockery. As for Alighieri, I have merely singled out what I have found most useful and have limited myself to books. Periodical references in the footnotes follow the abbreviated forms prescribed by the *PMLA International Bibliography*, except in a few cases where a full spelling seemed advisable. For Pound's works, I use shortened titles inside the text. Details for these titles are contained in the Select Bibliography. In every instance I use the most available edition of Pound's work, rather than a first edition. For the *Cantos*, I use the 1970 New Directions edition, which one hopes will remain the standard one for many years, for my direct citations. To distinguish between Dante and Pound, I use Roman numerals for canto numbers of the Italian work *(Par.* XXXI.13) and Arabic numerals for the modern work (Canto 3/11:15); the numbers after the slash mark are page numbers from the New Directions edition, followed by the Faber edition.

I am aware, thanks to a letter from Mary de Rachewiltz, that two fine Poundians have touched on this area. One is Hugh Kenner, whose essays have appeared in *Les Cahiers de l'Herne, 7* (1965), 473 ff., and in *Il Verri, 18* (1965), 35 ff. Another is Giovanni Giovannini, whose monograph *Ezra Pound and Dante*, though brief, puts Pound's early Dante training into a perspective with Longfellow, Rossetti, and other poets who were popular in his childhood. Doubtlessly the way that Pound discovered Dante is as important as the way that he uses him; this Professor Giovannini has already covered well, as has Glauco Cambon in his *Dante's Craft* (pp. 127 ff.). For an essay stressing the differences between the spatial concepts in the two writers, see Thomas Clark, *East-West Review, 1* (1964), 97 ff. Also useful for specific comparisons is Edwin Fussell, *Journal of Modern Literature, 1* (1970), 75 ff. Georg M. Gugelberger adds Cavalcanti in his study in *Paideuma, 2* (1973), 159 ff.

Others who have been helpful with comments or encouragement include Clark Emery, Carroll F. Terrell, José Vazquez-Amaral, Gerrit Lansing, and W. J. Dempsey. Carroll Terrell kindly drew the Chinese characters for the book, and both Janet Walker and Peter Li of Rutgers were extremely gracious in helping me interpret them. In my own training I had the good fortune to be directed to develop my interest in Pound by Norman Holmes Pearson. I also worked in the Yale Collection of American Literature under Donald Gallup—a collection to which I returned during the course of my study. I must thank the Yale and Cornell Libraries for granting me permission to quote from unpublished correspondence, as well as the Library of Congress, which allowed me the use of transcripts of Pound's Rome broadcasts.

As for the Italian side, I was fortunate enough to have studied under some of the greatest Dantistas of the century: T. G. Bergin and Erich Auerbach of Yale, Raffaele Spongano of Bologna, and Enrico de'Negri of Columbia. Furthermore, my teaching at Rutgers enabled me to avail myself of the intellectual companionship of Francis Fergusson and Glauco Cambon. I could never begin to say which perceptions I owe to whom regarding many passages, for conversations inside and outside of the classroom with these gentlemen were often more valuable than anything I read in critical texts.

Finally I must thank three people whose effect on this work was inestimable: Siegfried de Rachewiltz, who studied the Provençal lyric with me at Rutgers and who helped me to rediscover my interest in Pound; George Kearns, whose stimulating class on Pound at Rutgers gave me the specific idea for writing this book; and Ruth Wilhelm Southerland, who always supported my own belief that the best things of the past are forever new—an opinion hopefully borne out by the book in hand.

New Brunswick, N. J.
1974

ACKNOWLEDGEMENTS

Thanks are owed to the editors of the following journals which extended me permission to reprint essays, often in a somewhat emended form:*PMLA*, whose issue of March, 1974, contained Chapter 5 as the essay "Guido Cavalcanti as a Mask for Ezra Pound"; *Italian Quarterly*, whose Pound Issue (Spring, 1973) contained Chapter 8 under the title "Pound's Middle Cantos as an Analogue to Dante's *Purgatorio:* Purgatories Fictive and Real"; and *Paideuma*, whose Vol. 2, No. 2 (Fall, 1973) contained "Two Heavens of Light and Love: Paradise to Dante and to Pound," a reworking of Chapter 9.

I am also indebted to New Directions of New York and to Faber and Faber of London for permission to reprint citations from all of Pound's work under their copyright control (details to be found in Bibliography), as well as to Peter Owen Ltd. for its permission to reproduce extracts from *Spirit of Romance, Guide to Kulchur,* and *Pavannes and Divagations.*

Further, I must thank M. B. Yeats and the Macmillan Co. of Canada and the United States for permission to reprint from *A Vision* by W. B. Yeats; copyright 1937 by Macmillan Co., renewed 1965 by Bertha Georgie Yeats and Anne Butler Yeats. Also, M. B. Yeats for permission to reprint from *The Letters of W. B. Yeats,* published by Rupert Hart-Davis, 1954. Acknowledgement is also made to Viking Press for permission to quote from *Writers at Work,* 2d Series, introd. V. W. Brooks, 1963, extracts from the interview of Donald Hall that appeared originally in *Paris Review, 28* (1962), 22-51. Permission to translate from the Petrocchi-Ricci edition of the *Divina Commedia* was extended by Arnoldo Mondadori.

The art work of Cosimo Tura from the Room of Months in the Schifanoia Palace at Ferrara is reproduced with the permission of Alinari-Scala Publishers. The detail work of Dante appears with the permission of Scala Fine Arts Publishers of New York. Jacket design by Arline K. Thomson.

Dante and Pound
The Epic of Judgement

1

THE RHYTHMS OF TWO LIVES

What kind of man has the presumption to write an epic which attempts to judge his own age and the past? What kind of man purports to have the design by which he can put all things into order or at least into some coherent perspective? These are the two questions which lie at the heart of this study.

In attempting to compare Dante Alighieri and Ezra Pound, I have selected two unique subjects. In the three thousand years of extant European literature, these two men are the only ones who have taken the epic form, stripped it of much of its narrative trappings, and emphasized its potential for qualitative analysis. In one sense all epics pass moral judgements of some kind. No doubt the ephebes in the circle around Pericles could observe clear-cut distinctions in virtue among the warriors of the *Iliad*. Certainly the *Odyssey*, especially as it was rendered into a twentieth century idiom by James Joyce, is a work in which the surviving Odysseus is measured against his worthless companions, who fall prey to the many vices that dot the road home to Ithaca. And surely Vergil, who adapted the Greek epic tradition to his own ends, was trying to establish the *virtus* of Aeneas against the temptations of Dido on the journey from Troy to Rome. But an entire poem in which judgement is present at every step of the way and where the intellect delights in morality far more than in narrative line—this seems to be the invention of the Florentine.[1] Only Pound in the intervening centuries had the courage to try to duplicate the feat.

If we look at the lives of the two men, we find not only some striking similarities, but we also learn something about the kind of man who attempts the cosmic vision. Dante was born in 1265 under Gemini, "the sign that follows Taurus," as he himself tells us in *Paradiso* XXII.106-117.[2] He was the son of Gabriella (Bella) and Alighiero di Bellincione degli Alighieri, a man who traced his name and roots to the noble Aldighiero family of Ferrara. A Ferrarese lady named Aldighiera had married Dante's great-great-grandfather, Cacciaguida, and the letter *d* was later dropped from the family name. Cacciaguida relates these facts himself when he appears in the Heaven of Mars as a martyred crusader (*Paradiso* XV.130 ff.):

> To such a quiet, such a lovely life
> as citizen, to a citizenry so true,
> to such a hostelry that was ever sweet
> Maria gave me—called to in your highest cries;
> and in that ancient Baptistery of yours
> I became both Christian and Cacciaguida.
> Moronto was my brother, and Eliseo;
> my lady came to me from the Valley Po;
> and your surname thus was taken from her.
> Later on, I followed Conrad, Holy Emperor,
> and he girded me as one of his militia,
> and through good works I rose up in the ranks.
> Behind him I opposed that heathen evil
> which, through the blame of your silent pastors,
> works to overthrow what is rightly yours.
> Off there, at the hands of that accursed race,
> I was stripped away from the swath of your lying world,
> the love of which corrupts many a soul,
> and from that martyrdom to this peace I came.

Despite his claim to noble origins, Dante (or Durante, to use his full name) was not a rich man. When Alighiero died, he left Dante and his half-brother Francesco some land outside of Florence and a city house in the San Martino quarter of town, near the modern Via Dante Alighieri.[3] The father seems to have been constantly hovering on the verge of bankruptcy, and if we can believe the vicious exchange of satiric poems between Forese Donati and Dante,[4] both father and son were involved in moneylending. Some scattered documents show that during the early portion of his life Dante himself was much troubled by indebtedness. This lack of a business sense as well as his lust (which is pointed out by Boccaccio in his *Life of Dante*) seem to have been the Florentine's major flaws.[5]

We might term the first phase of Dante's life "The Young Life," as suggested by the title of his early work, *La Vita Nuova*. This phase would extend up to the death of his beloved Beatrice on June 8, 1290. During his youth Dante mastered the various parts of the medieval trivium and quadrivium, as his later works show. His fascination for lyric poetry began at least as early as the age of eighteen, as he tells us in Chapter III of the *Vita Nuova*. Legend has it that he did some work at the University of Bologna, perhaps around the year 1287, but there is no written proof.

If we accept Chapter II of the *Vita Nuova* as biographical fact, we know that Dante first met the girl whom he was to immortalize as his celestial guide at a party in the home of her father when he was nine years old. We have the further words of Boccaccio to vouch for the identification of this Beatrice (the name stems from the Latin *beatrix*, "bestower of blessings") as Bice dei Portinari, daughter of the wealthy merchant Folco and later the wife of Simone dei Bardi.[6] Indeed, if we try to take her as a pure symbol and reject her as a real woman, as Pound was tempted to do in his revised notations of *The Spirit of Romance* in 1929 (p. 126), she would be the sole fictional contemporary character in the entire *Comedy*.

At some point Dante himself married Gemma of the Donati clan, as had been prearranged by his father. She bore him two sons, Iacopo and Pietro (and possibly a third named Giovanni), and a daughter, Antonia, who is often identified as a certain Sister Beatrice, who retired to a monastery in Ravenna late in Dante's life.[7] In all of his work, there is no mention of his father or mother or wife;[8] but similarly in Pound's *Cantos,* there are only oblique references to Dorothy Pound (or Olga Rudge), as in "say to La Cara: amo" (Canto 76/459:488). Pound said to John Drummond in 1932 that "personal love poetry [was] neither in Cantos nor in any Epos . . . even (say) Beatrice in the *Commedia*" (*Letters*, p. 240).

Dante's intellectual growth was greatly influenced by three men: Brunetto Latini, a poet and professor who appears among the homosexuals in *Inferno* XV; Guido Guinizelli, a Bolognese judge who wrote the philosophical poems which provided a framework for Dante's circle; and Guido Cavalcanti, a wealthy older poet who befriended the youthful Alighieri after the dissemination of Dante's first poem about Beatrice, as we are told in *Vita Nuova* III. We shall return to all of these later.

The decade or so from the death of Beatrice in 1290 to Dante's exile in 1302 forms the second period of the poet's life, when he plunged into the social and political activities of his city. The fact that Dante was very much a man-about-town is revealed in the flashing exchanges of poems with Cavalcanti, Cino of Pistoia, Lapo Gianni, Dante of Maiano, and the scurrilous Cecco Angiolieri of Siena, although that exchange may have taken place somewhat later. We know that Dante was already famous as a lyric poet in his late twenties because in *Paradiso* VIII.31 he encounters Charles Martel, who cites the poem *Voi che 'ntendendo il terzo ciel movete* from *Convivio* II. Charles Martel, the son of King Charles II of Naples, visited Florence in 1294, the same period that Dante was probably putting the finishing touches on the *Vita Nuova*.[9] The Florentine was thus blessed with early luck in his writing.

In 1295 Dante took an important step in another direction when he joined the Guild of Apothecaries and Physicians, which included painters and other artists. He thereby qualified for a position as one of the Priors or ruling members of the Florentine government.[10] During the next few years Dante's name crops up in a variety of places concerning the governing of the commune, and his success culminated with his election in June, 1300, as one of the Priors.

But success carried with it danger and possible disaster. For the Italy of the early fourteenth century was still involved in repercussions of the Guelph-Ghibelline struggle that eventually brought about Dante's expulsion. In his short account of Dante's life contained in *The Spirit of Romance,* Pound sums up the differences between the two political parties succinctly: "The Ghibelline party, ruined in the year of Dante's birth, stood in theory for 'law, authority, the empire, and the older aristocracy'; the Guelph party for the citizens, the Church, liberty, and Italy" (p. 118).

The rivalry, which began in Austria between the Welfs (in Italian, *Guelfi*) and the Waiblings (or *Ghibellini*), was furthered through the strong actions of the allegedly heretical, revolutionary Holy Roman Emperor Frederick II. It was continued by his son Manfred, who was soundly beaten with his Ghibelline followers in the famous Battle of Benevento in 1266 by Charles of Anjou, who became King Charles I of Naples. Earlier up in the north, in 1260, the Guelphs had been decisively beaten by the Sienese and the Florentine Ghibellines under the command of Count Guido Novello, with the fiery

Farinata degli Uberti of *Inferno* X in the fore. But after Benevento the Guelphs were restored to power. Dante himself fought in the battle of Campaldino in 1289, which further suppressed the Ghibellines in the Arno, at least for the time.

In the period of Dante's political activism, the Guelph majority had splintered into two factions led by the Cerchi and the Donati clans.[11] The Donati (and it must be remembered that Gemma, Dante's wife, belonged to this family) were pro-Papal and were called the Blacks. They were captained by the cruel and self-willed Corso Donati, a man who is referred to only obliquely in Dante's epic. The Cerchi followers were called the Whites, and were led by Dante's great friend, Guido Cavalcanti.

When Dante was elevated to his highest role in the Florentine government, the feud between Corso and Guido had reached such proportions that the bloodshed and harassment could be stopped only by exile. As a result, the Blacks were sent inland to a mountain redoubt, and the Whites were banished to the little town of Sarzana on the Ligurian coast, to the northwest of the city. Sarzana was malaria-ridden in the summer, and Guido contracted the disease. He was recalled to his native city for treatment, but too late. He died of the fever in August of 1300 and was buried in the Church of Santa Reparata, now the famous Santa Maria dei Fiori. His role in Pound's and Dante's careers will be considered at length later, for he was extremely important to both.

In 1301 as trouble between Florence and Rome reached a crescendo, the Whites, who were in control of the city, decided to send an embassy to Pope Boniface VIII to ward off the incursion of Charles of Valois, the brother of the French king Philip the Fair, who was making rapid strides through northern Italy. Dante may have been one of three men sent to see the Pope at his residence in Anagni. If we can believe Dino Compagni's *Cronica* II.4, the complex Boniface is reported to have assured the ambassadors: ''I tell you truthfully that I have no intention other than what is conducive to your peace. Go back, two of you; and take along my blessing if you see to it that my will is obeyed.'' Dante, according to this single account, was detained. With promises of amity to all, Charles triumphantly entered the city by the Arno and Dante learned that he was accused of barratry (the sale of public office), as well as other public crimes. Ironically, these sins are the very ones that Dante rails against most violently as in *Inferno* XXI and XXII, and that Pound himself bewails in Canto 77/470:500:

> lacking that treasure of honesty
> which is the treasure of states
> and the dog-damn wop is not, save by exception,
> honest in administration any more than the briton is truthful.

Dante was not immediately exiled. He could, upon the payment of a fine and the restoration of some allegedly stolen goods, come home after a two-year period, but he was barred from holding any future offices. When he did not answer the accusation, he was handed a savage second sentence on March 10, 1302, which threatened that he would be burned alive if he ever reappeared on Florentine soil.

Thus begins the third phase of Dante's life: the early exile from 1302 to 1308. We can best evaluate this period by listening to the poet himself speaking in the *Convivio* I.3:

> Since it was the pleasure of the citizens of the most beautiful and most famous daughter of Rome—I mean Florence—to toss me away from her sweet bosom, in which I was born and nurtured up to the apex of my life and in which, with full peace, I wish with all my heart to rest my weary soul... I have gone, wandering, almost begging. . . . Truly I am a bark without a sail and a rudder, carried to various ports and shores and strands by a dry wind that sprays a grievous poverty. . . .

Even more dramatic is the passage in *Paradiso* XVII.55 ff. where the poet speaks through the persona of his ancestor Cacciaguida, first portraying a picture of old-time Florence in terms of ancient Rome, and then verifying the dark prophecy about Dante's fate that has been accruing through the course of the poem:

> You will be leaving everything you love
> most dearly; this is arrow number one
> by which the bow of banishment impales.
> You will test indeed the salty taste
> of someone else's bread; you'll find how hard
> is the up and down upon another's stairs *(scale)*.
> And what will weigh your shoulders down the most
> will be that evil, godforsaken crew
> who will tumble with you down into this vale:
> all of them ingrates, mad and godless,
> ranking themselves against you—but wait a bit!
> They—not you—will find their temples red.
> A single trial will summon forth the proof

of their bestiality; and you'll be very glad
to form a party of yourself alone.
Your very first refuge, your first hostelry
will issue from the courtesy of that great Lombard
whose shield has the holy bird over some stairs *(scala)*.
Over you he'll bestow such a benign regard
that between the asking and the doing between you both
the time will be so prompt it will make the others slow.
At his place you will see a lad who at birth
was beamed on by a very potent star
so that all his undertakings will be noted.
But the folks around him don't know this yet
because of his young age, for a mere nine years
have turned their circlings around his head.
But before the Gascon Pope frigs our great Henry
out will flow tales about his virtues,
about his great disdain for loot and labors.
The magnificence of him will be cast abroad
and soon will change his detractors' tongues
so that even they won't be mute about his deeds.
So wait for him! and for his benefits.
Through him will come a change for many men,
transformations of states of rich and low.

    The "great Lombard" is one of the members of the Della Scala family, whose name is punned on twice with the meaning "stairs"; if we can believe Boccaccio, the exact man was Alberto.[12] The Wunderkind who is described in terms of Vergil's Messianic *Eclogue* IV is undoubtedly Can Grande (Big Dog), to whom Dante addressed his famous Epistle X. The canine part of his name suggests a correlation with the avenging Greyhound of *Inferno* I.

    And so began the long years of banishment and despair. It is impossible to know exactly where the poet went and with whom he stayed, but some of the people mentioned in letters and in other sources are Scarpetta Ordelaffi of Forlì, Moroello Malaspina, and the Countess Gherardesca di Battifolle of the mountainous Casentino region to the north of Florence. Dante undoubtedly revisited Bologna, and he may well, as both Boccaccio and Leonardo Bruni suggest, have visited Paris.[13] At this time, as Michele Barbi conjectures, he probably wrote the *Convivio* and the *De vulgari eloquentia* as attempts to justify himself and to widen his intellectual reputation.[14] Doubtlessly it was also at this time that he began his masterwork, selecting the Jubilee Year of 1300 as the time for the vision of his poem. And no doubt the writing of this epic, especially the early Hell parts, helped to sustain him during this difficult period when he himself seemed beset with infernal pain. After 1308, however, things seemed to brighten. The promising Henry of Luxemburg ascended to the throne of the Holy Roman Empire as Henry VII amid jubilation on the part of those who desired a strong imperial thrust. In 1310 he entered Italy, determined to assert his authority. Dante, among others, rejoiced in words that recall Pound's own rhetoric when directed toward Mussolini or other rulers who "make it new." In Epistle V.1, Dante said:

> "Behold, now the time is right!" which shows the standards of peace and consolation on the rise. Now a new day is gleaming, showing a dawning in the East, which is driving away the shadows of a long tribulation. Now the orient breeze is livelier. The sky grows rosy with its lips comforting the world with auspices of sweet serenity. And we, who have kept long vigil in the desert, shall see our long-awaited joy.

In Epistle VII.2 Dante calls Henry "our sun" and "the minister of God, the son of the Church, and the sustainer of the glory of Rome." Acting somewhat the way Pound did in his *Jefferson and/or Mussolini*, Dante transfers the rhetoric usually attached to the Celestial Messiah Christ when he says in Epistle VII.2: "My spirit rose up in me when in silence I could whisper to myself: 'Behold the lamb of God; behold him who takes away the sins of the world.' "

Hand in hand with this adoration of the Monarch went a stream of bitter invective directed against his former fellow-citizens:

> O godforsaken spawn of Fiesole! You barbarism punished a second time! Does the foretaste strike so little fear in you? Indeed, I think I see you shaking and sleepless, even if you do feign a little hope with your looks and your lying words. Often you bolt up in your sleep, trembling with premonitions that pour over you.

In Epistle VII.8, he openly urged Henry to "overthrow this Goliath," heaping on the names of all the worst monsters and dating his letter "the first year of the blessed incursion of the divine Henry into Italy." Similarly Pound years later was to proudly date his letters with the initials E. F. (Era Fascista) and Roman numerals marking the years of Mussolini's rule. The Florentines were so furious with Dante's behavior that they omitted his name from the Reform of Baldo d'Aguglione, in which they recalled many other banished Whites from exile.

But unfortunately for Dante, the dream of an Earthly Paradise under Holy Germanic rule was not to be realized. Henry VII literally sank in the quagmire of Italian politics. Before he could reach Florence, he was drawn into a succession of squabbles among Milan, Cremona, and Brescia. By the time he finally reached Florence, he and his troops seemed to be suffering from physical as well as mental exhaustion. He laid siege to the city, but that supposedly degenerate town pulled itself together and successfully withstood the attack. Emperor Henry retreated, and, coming down with a fever, died soon after on August 24, 1313. Dante had undoubtedly lost a great deal of faith in the Swabian even before that time, just as Pound foresaw the end of Mussolini long before he was hanging by the heels in the square at Milan. In fact, Pound's opening line of the *Pisan Cantos* might well have expressed Dante's own dejection: "The enormous tragedy of the dream in the peasant's bent shoulders."

Still, the imperial forces did not collapse with this loss. Indeed, there arose a far more efficient tormentor of Florence, a man named Uguccione della Faggiuola, who harassed the men of the Arno with great success. And after him there was the celebrated Can Grande himself, who was now old enough to carry the burden that Cacciaguida set for him in the *Paradiso* speech. In one sense all of these men were failures; but in another they were the groundlayers for the eventual outcome that Dante longed for: the separation of Church and State, and the creation of a united Italy.

The last period of Dante's life consists of the years from 1314 to 1321. We do not know many details about these years, but we suppose from his own statements that the majority of the time was spent with Can Grande and the Scaligers at Verona and with Guido Novello da Polenta, a nobleman of Ravenna. Of datable items, we know that in 1314 Dante wrote an impassioned letter, Epistle VIII, on the death of Pope Clement V, begging the Italian cardinals to elect a fellow countryman and thus restore an Italian element to the Church, which was still undergoing the Babylonian Captivity at Avignon. But that fractious group, still under the influence of Philip the Fair of France, chose a Frenchman, Jacques d'Euse, who was installed as Pope John XXII.

One year later the city of Florence at last relented and told Dante that he could return—with the stipulation that he come on St. John's Day and offer an oblation as a humble penitent. Dante's scornful

Epistle IX, written to "A Florentine Friend," refuses to obey the humiliating terms and thus closes the matter once and for all. On November 6, 1315, he was once again condemned to death if he was ever found on Florentine soil.

Dante's stay with the Scaligers of Verona was probably not as placid as Cacciaguida foretold, for the embittered poet could not take subjection easily. One anecdote that circulated found Can Grande saying to his famous guest: "Why is the jester, who's an ignorant man, so sought after, while you, the great and brilliant Dante, are ignored?" The Florentine replied: "Like manners are the strongest bond."[15]

Undoubtedly the beautiful city of Ravenna, celebrated by Pound for its mosaics and the Tomb of Galla Placidia, was a more hospitable place. From here Dante could travel and lecture, writing on technical matters as in the *Questio de aqua et terra,* which is believed to have been delivered as a lecture in Verona in 1320. It is in Ravenna that Dante died on September 13 or 14, 1321, and is still entombed. Giovanni Villani tells us that the poet succumbed to a fever on returning from an embassy to Venice in the service of Guido Novello da Polenta, and that he was buried in the garments of a poet and philosopher.[16] Boccaccio and Leonardo Bruni tell us that the Bolognese scholar Giovanni del Virgilio, who had exchanged Latin *Eclogues* with Dante, wrote the epitaph and that Guido Novello delivered the eulogy.[17] Bruni says that during the papal reign of Leo X, the Florentines tried to carry the bones back to the banks of the Arno, but they were repelled, and a perpetual guard was established at the Tomb near the Church of San Francesco to forbid the poet's native city from ever winning back her most famous literary son.[18]

At first glance the life of Ezra Pound may seem to be quite different from Dante's, but it obeys the same general pattern of youthful separation from native land, embracing of foreign and even treasonable causes, attempted reconciliation, and final separation, although in Pound's case the last severing proved to be rather amicable. Both Dante and Pound were declared traitors by their native states, both were threatened with death, and both reacted with a mixture of love and hatred that took its finest form as some of the world's greatest poetry.

Ezra Pound was born on October 30, 1885, in as American a place as one could ask for: the little town of Hailey, Idaho, where his father, Homer Loomis Pound, was superintending the United States Land Office.[19] Through his mother, Isabel, Ezra was related to the Westons, a family that had come to America on the *Lion* shortly after the sailing of the *Mayflower*. He refers to them in Canto 62/341:357, connecting his forebears with the Adams family. His paternal grandfather was Thaddeus Coleman Pound, a man whom Ezra proudly remembered under the fictionalized name of Thadeus Cuthberton Weight (already an economic pun on his family name!) in his veiled autobiography, *Indiscretions or, Une Revue de Deux Mondes*, which was published in Paris by William Bird in 1923 and reprinted in the more recent *Pavannes and Divagations* (pp. 3 ff.). Thaddeus was not only a pioneering railway-builder but he also experimented in monetary reform by issuing scrip money when he was blocked by the banks and monopolistic interests. Thus Pound's forebears were firmly Yankee.

Ezra was taken east in his infancy and really grew up in Wyncote, a suburb of Philadelphia, where his father was an assistant assayer for the Government Mint downtown. In a much-quoted interview of Pound by Donald Hall that appeared in the *Paris Review* in 1962 (*28*, 22-51), Pound describes very vividly the childhood vision of half-naked men shoveling coal into the fires at the coining house. Money, from the start, was an important factor in his life, if only because he grew up in a house where the making of it was literally the source of income.

Pound's education was begun at the University of Pennsylvania in 1901, but after two years he transferred to the more rural Hamilton College in Clinton, New York. There he had the good fortune to meet Joseph Ibbotson, who taught Old and Middle English, and William P. Shepard, the well-known Professor of Romance Languages, who fostered Pound's interest in medieval literature by teaching him Old Provençal, as well as other languages. It was here that Ezra began to develop his interest in Dante. On his return for graduate studies at Pennsylvania in 1905, he was taught by three professors who influenced him further: Cornelius Weygandt, Felix Schelling, and Hugo Rennert.[20] Rennert's work on Lope de Vega and Spanish literature in general nurtured Pound's dream of doing a doctoral dissertation in Comparative Romance Literature in the Middle Ages and the Renaissance. This dream was never realized, although the publication of *The Spirit of Romance,* through the further encouragement of Ernest Rhys, was some recompense for the labor.

At Penn Pound associated with two young people who were to play important roles with him in the formation of twentieth-century poetry: William Carlos Williams, who was studying medicine, and Hilda Doolittle (the future H. D.), who was the daughter of a professor of astronomy. He was dating regularly a girl from Trenton named Mary S. Moore, who received the dedication of the 1909 edition of *Personae,* but their romance never led to marriage. Another woman of this period who exerted a strong influence on Pound was Katherine Ruth Heyman, a concert pianist who was considerably older than the tall, red-haired poet. Pound's interest in music is a constant feature of his career, for besides Miss Heyman, he was friendly with Walter Morse Rummel, Olga Rudge, and George Antheil in later years. In the thirties, he held many musical concerts in Rapallo, wrote two operas (*Le Testament de Villon* and *Cavalcanti*), and went so far as to print medieval notations from the troubadours in Canto 91 and a violin transcription of Janequin's *Song of the Birds* in Canto 75. Pound dreamed of restoring the relationship between lyric poetry and music that he felt was lost after Henry Lawes and Thomas Campion, knowing that Dante in the *De vulgari* had discussed the necessary balance between music and words.

In the summer of 1907 Pound was ready to try his hand at teaching. He wrangled a job at Wabash College in Crawfordsville, Indiana, and began what he hoped would be an idyllic existence in the American heartland. The poet's affected manner—his cane, his floppy hat, his flashy clothes, his smoking, and his tendency to spout foreign phrases—was not, however, calculated to endear him to the Hoosiers. The story about his keeping a down-and-out actress in his room all night has been told in many versions.[21] All that matters is that this affair helped to terminate his position at the school, and he was suddenly forced to dream up a new career. The incident filled him with revulsion toward American "learneries" and "beaneries," and the general American refusal to distinguish between a man's private and public lives. Pound felt inextricably cut off from his countrymen, and he thus embarked on an exile that was to last, with interruptions in 1910 and 1939, for many years.

The poet had been to Europe before—with his aunt Frances Weston, his father, and by himself. This time he found himself drawn

to the two countries that would dominate his future life: England and
Italy. He went to Venice first, where he was later to picture himself as
a poor outcast in Canto 3/11:15:

> I sat on the Dogana's steps
> For the gondolas cost too much, that year,
> And there were not "those girls," there was one face,
> And the Buccentoro twenty yards off, howling "Stretti."

It was here in 1908 that he arranged for the printing of his first book of
poems, *A Lume Spento*, a title which he took from Dante's
Purgatorio III.132, meaning "With Tapers Quenched," as he rendered it on the title page. The phrase refers to the premature death of
the flashing Manfred, son of Emperor Frederick II, and the import
was transferred by Pound to William Brooke Smith, a young and
talented painter from Philadelphia whose death from consumption
the poet mourned even years later in a letter to Williams (*Letters*, p.
165). The despair in Pound's own situation as fledgling exile and
insecure artist can be sensed in the following lines from Canto
76/460:489:

> shd/I chuck the lot into the tide-water?
> le bozze "A Lume Spento"/

Fortunately he did not throw the proofs (bozze) into the canal, but
went on to London.

 There he soon fell into the whirl of social and artistic life that kept
him occupied for several years. One of his first friends was the
bookdealer Elkin Mathews, who published much of Pound's early
work and introduced him around. Very soon he met Olivia Shakespear, who was a friend of William Butler Yeats, the man who Pound
said later was his entire reason for coming to London.[22] Olivia made
the introduction that was so important for the course of modern
poetry. She also introduced Ezra to her daughter, Dorothy, whom he
married in 1914. Pound met many of the other established men of
letters in London literary circles: Ernest Rhys, Arthur Symons, W.
H. Hudson, G. K. Chesterton, Laurence Binyon, and Robert
Bridges. He was able to say in retrospect in Canto 82/523:558:

> Swinburne my only miss
> and I didn't know he'd been to see Landor.

Two other men who had an important impact on the young writer were T. E. Hulme, whose philosophical ideas bore fruit in Pound's part in the Imagist movement, and A. R. Orage, the editor of the *New Age*, who practically kept Pound alive by offering him small editorial jobs, especially after World War I. Hulme fed the aesthetic fires of the poet; Orage kept them burning by supplying hard cash. Orage also introduced Ezra to Major C. H. Douglas, whose ideas on Social Credit were to supply the poet with an economic framework for the early parts of his major work.

After a brief visit to America in 1910-11, Pound returned to London and fell back in with Ford Madox (Hueffer) Ford, the novelist and editor of the *English Review*, whose affair with Violet Hunt became a sensation. The genial Ford considered Pound a bit strange, largely because of his American affectations, but in some of his many memoirs, he looks back on Ezra with affection and amusement.[23] In a letter to Lady Gregory written on December 10, 1909, Yeats himself called Pound a "queer creature," but added that he "has become really a great authority on the troubadours, [and] has I think got closer to the right sort of music for poetry than Mrs. Emery."[24]

Pound met many other newcomers like Robert Frost and D. H. Lawrence (both of whom he later regarded rather negatively), as well as that grand old man of letters Henry James, an earlier expatriate for whom he wrote one of his finest tributes (*Essays*, pp. 295 ff.).

In 1912 Pound accepted the job as European poetry editor for a new magazine called *Poetry*, which was based in Chicago and edited by Harriet Monroe, an American spinster with a predilection for American works. She gave the expatriate an opportunity to exert his taste upon the next decade, even if she was often in stern disagreement with it. Her fondness for Sandburg and her aversion to Eliot are now almost legendary, but she did publish "The Love Song of J. Alfred Prufrock," as well as many other classics of the early twentieth century, with thanks to Pound's prodding. In the March 1913 issue of *Poetry* appeared an article by Pound called "Imagisme" in which he laid the groundwork for the much-debated Imagist movement.[25] Nobody knows who began this movement, or if it really existed, but T. E. Hulme is generally considered the spiritual father through such writings as *Speculations*; Pound himself nominated Ford Madox Ford through his conversations. At its height around 1914 it was composed of Hilda Doolittle, Richard Aldington, John

Gould Fletcher, F. S. Flint, and various poets from Pound's anthology *Des Imagistes*, including the eccentric, cigar-smoking American heiress Amy Lowell, whom Pound envisioned as the Maecenas of this new school. When Miss Lowell insisted that she did not have the money to support Pound in buying out the *Mercure de France* and that she had her own ideas about the democratic process in the selection of material for her forthcoming anthologies, Pound withdrew from her and the "Amygism" movement in disgust (*Letters*, pp. 38 ff.). His later letters to her are full of vitriole, and the remark in Canto 77/469:489 about the artist "Gaudier's eye on the telluric mass of Miss Lowell" shows the way that he retained his distaste.

Actually, much of Pound's venom was directed toward the world in general, for in the same year that Miss Lowell reappeared in London, 1914, Pound produced with his friend, the painter and writer Wyndham Lewis, a magazine called BLAST which, living up to its name, lashed out at prevailing British social and intellectual institutions. The aesthetic excuse for the magazine was that it was promoting a new movement called Vorticism, but the review, which lasted for only two issues, was really an expression of the editors' disgust toward modern society, especially its disregard for art.

Also during the London years Pound was in correspondence with Harriet Shaw Weaver, the editor of the *New Freewoman* (later called the *Egoist*), and with Margaret Anderson and Jane Heap of the *Little Review* in Chicago. These were the primary outlets for his own work and that of two of the finest talents of the period: a young American out of Harvard named Thomas Stearns Eliot and a witty Irishman named James Joyce, who was living in a self-imposed exile in Trieste. Pound's loyal support of both was great in the face of stolid disagreement. Indeed, one wonders on reading Pound's correspondence if either name would be known today had Pound not been on the London scene. The most influential critics of the day honored such men as Rupert Brooke, G. K. Chesterton, H. G. Wells, the Bloomsbury group, Tennyson, and others whom Pound detested much in the same way that Dante spurned Guittone d'Arezzo, Bonaguinta da Lucca, and other members of the preceding generation. Indeed Pound's Imagist and Vorticist movements were in some ways parallels to Dante's *dolce stil nuovo*, with the feeling that poets can work more effectively if they move in groups.

When World War I broke out, Pound went off frequently to Coleman's Hatch, Sussex, to act as secretary to Yeats. In Canto 83/533:569, Pound describes the marvelous sound of Yeats creating a poem downstairs:

> so that I recalled the noise in the chimney
> as it were the wind in the chimney
>   but was in reality Uncle William
> downstairs composing
> that had made a great Peeeeacock
>   in the proide ov his oiye
>   had made a great peeeeeeecock in the . . .
> made a great peacock
>   in the proide of his oyyee

While Pound, as an American, was exempt from military service at the start of the war, he watched most of his European friends trudging off to fight what he increasingly came to look upon as a vicious, useless campaign. He was especially shocked by the death of the young French sculptor Henri Gaudier-Brzeska, from whom he had expected a brilliant future. Canto 16/71:75 describes the impact of this period upon the author succinctly:

> And Henri Gaudier went to it,
>   and they killed him,
> And killed a good deal of sculpture,
> And ole T.E.H. he went to it,
> With a lot of books from the library,
> London Library, and a shell buried 'em in a dug-out,
> And the Library expressed its annoyance.

Years later in the biographical note that opens his *Selected Poems,* Pound was to say of his wartime activities: I "began investigation of causes of war, to oppose same." This investigation took the form of discussions with Orage about the economic ideas of Major Douglas, for Pound came increasingly to believe that all wars are waged for money and that moral issues are entirely secondary. Certainly he felt no love for the British imperial machine.

The war ended, but peace brought no real improvement in the lot of Pound or his friends. Eliot was trapped in a bank working at starvation wages, unable to publish unless Pound sat on Harriet Monroe, Harriet Shaw Weaver, or some other editor. Joyce was starving in Trieste, working desultorily in a language school and desperately in need of eye operations. Pound himself reported later that he made only 42 pounds during a one-year stretch in London.[26] Feeling that life in England was impossible, he decided to leave for Paris, which was very much alive with such talents as Picasso, Picabia, and Cocteau.

The Parisian period was rather brief, however, extending only from late 1920 to 1924. Still, it was a brilliant time, seeing the production of much of the finest work of Eliot, Joyce, and Pound, and introducing two promising newcomers, Ernest Hemingway and E. E. Cummings, who quickly became warm friends of Ezra's.[27] It was then that Pound met his second female nemesis, whom he called among other things "oedipus Gertie" (*Letters*, p. 227): Gertrude Stein.

During the Paris phase Pound became friendly with Olga Rudge, an American violinist who joined him in a love affair that extended into the poet's old age. She bore him a daughter, Maria or Mary, in Bressanone in the Italian Tyrol on July 9, 1925, who was sent to live in the town of Gais with a peasant family named Marcher, who had lost a baby on the day of Mary's birth. Mary became a translator and poet in her own right; she married the noted Egyptologist Boris de Rachewiltz, and received her father in their castle, Brunnenburg, at Merano when he was released from American confinement.[28] Back in Paris on September 10, 1926, Dorothy gave birth to a son, who was christened Omar Shakespear Pound. Later Ezra remarked jestfully in conversation that the boy "carries the names of three of the world's greatest poets" (the Omar signifying Homer more than Khayyam). He was placed in the custody of Olivia Shakespear and grew up in England.

Gradually Pound became annoyed by the whirl of life in Paris. Since he was now seriously engaged in writing his epic, he needed a more quiet, restful place to work in. Furthermore, he was becoming more and more interested in politics. France, in his eyes, did not seem to be doing anything as interesting as the Russia reported to him by Lincoln Steffens or, even more so, the Italy which seemed to be enjoying a Renaissance after the march of Mussolini on Rome in 1922. As a result, he once again decided to move—this time to the tranquil Ligurian town of Rapallo, to the east of Genoa. Although he returned to Paris frequently for musical occasions, Rapallo was to be his home for many years to come.

The Rapallo years saw an increased productivity in Pound's creative work. In 1926 he published his *Personae: Collected Poems*, which was in actuality a restricted selection of much of his finest lyric work to that time. Until the year 1939 he was working feverishly on his *Cantos*, moving up to number 71 when the war broke out. Except for the satiric Alfred Venison poems, which were reprinted from the *New English Weekly* in the 1949 edition of *Personae* (pp. 257 ff.), he was now exclusively an epic poet.

During this period Pound was much occupied in correspondence with people like Mary Barnard, who was to translate Sappho very beautifully; with W. H. D. Rouse, who was working on Homer's *Odyssey;* and with Laurence Binyon, who was rendering the *Divine Comedy* in an English terza rima that Pound found highly appealing. There were many letters to friends—Hemingway, Harriet Monroe, E. E. Cummings, William Carlos Williams, and others. There were visits from such people as Yeats, Louis Zukofsky, Basil Bunting, and Gerhart Hauptmann. But still, in reviewing the correspondence, one notes a sense of alienation in the writing, as well as a certain frustration at being removed from good libraries and the sophisticated centers of talk that he had for so long taken for granted.[29]

Meanwhile Pound's economic interests had intensified, and he saw a new possibility for action in Mussolini's programs. He met the Duce only one time, but that encounter is recorded in Canto 41/202:210, where Mussolini, flipping through the poem, says, "But this is amusing" with a Romagnole accent:

"Ma qvesto,"
        said the Boss, "è divertente."
catching the point before the aesthetes had got there;
Having drained off the muck by Vada
From the marshes, by Circeo, where no one else wd. have drained it.
Waited 2000 years, ate grain from the marshes;
Water supply for ten million, another one million "*vani*"
that is rooms for people to live in.
        XI of our era.

The other primary allusion to Mussolini occurs in Canto 93/626:659, where a question that is mentioned several times before in Italian ("Why do you want to put your ideas into order?") is answered by Pound ("Because of my poem"):

or "Perché" said the Boss
"vuol mettere le sue idee in ordine?"
        "Pel mio poema."

Despite the briefness of the encounter, Pound was convinced that the Boss was leading Italy on the path toward beneficial social and economic reforms, whereas Roosevelt, Churchill, and the French authorities could only rely on another war to get their people out of the throes of the Depression. He thus bombarded friends and politicians with urgent notes about enacting money reforms, usually promoting the ideas of Major Douglas and Silvio Gesell (*Letters*, pp. 239 ff.).

Pound's frenzy reached such a pitch that in 1939, when the thunderclouds were gathering over Europe, he returned to America in an attempt to talk politics with Franklin Delano Roosevelt. As might have been expected, the President was too busy, and thus Pound had to content himself with a lunch with Henry Wallace, the Secretary of Agriculture, whom he met through Paul de Kruif. He had some snippets of conversation with Senators William E. Borah, J. H. Bankhead, Harry F. Byrd, Burton K. Wheeler, and Congressmen Jerry Voorhis and "Uncle George" Holden Tinkham. Pathetically ineffectual as these encounters were, they are duly recorded in the *Cantos*, where they are offered as proofs of Pound's caring for his native land. Ezra went on to Hamilton College, where he received an honorary degree and irritated a number of people with his impertinence toward another commencement speaker, the news commentator H. V. Kaltenborn. He returned to Italy feeling bitter and disgruntled.

When the United States entered World War II, Pound considered returning to his homeland, but his father had retired to Rapallo, and Ezra claimed that there was a mix-up with the American authorities over his passport, although this report has been challenged. At any rate, he stayed primarily in Rapallo with Dorothy, often making the short trip to Sant'Ambrogio to be with Olga Rudge. His primary intellectual contact during the war was George Santayana. Pound saw the retired professor of philosophy on his visits to Rome, where Ezra had begun to lecture on the air. Although many people were shocked when Pound took to broadcasting regularly over Radio Rome, this action seemed to spring out of his conviction that American politicians were no longer honoring the spirit or even the letter of the United States Constitution. His broadcasts were prefaced by the remark that he was speaking of his own volition as an American citizen and was not in any sense an official spokesman for the Mussolini government, but the slant in the oratory could easily lead one to doubt the veracity of the claim.[30] The talks, often badly transcribed and poorly monitored because of weather difficulties, are on deposit at the Library of Congress. In them one senses the tragic condition of an intelligent mind caring passionately about the world, and tortured by the very intensity of the emotions which are energizing the intellect. There are long flights of fantasy punctuated by vituperative gasps, as in the speech for February 3, 1942: "'a prospect of a 30 years war is not one to arouse mirth and hilarity, even in a flighty chicken hearted and irresponsible people such as the United States of Americans. You are in it and Lord knows whose is it trying to get you out." (I have left the errors intact, for Pound's Uncle Ez drawl also caused some trouble for the transcriber.) In all the talks, there was a desperate attempt to cling to his American roots: "Ezra Pound speaking from Europe for the American heritage" (March 26, 1942) and to claim his devotion for "what the United States Constitution was" (April 9, 1942); but in the main the speeches are characterized by an obsessive drive that is the inevitable prelude to tragedy.

In 1943 when the United States Government took the action of informing Pound that he was engaged in treasonable conduct, the poet replied that he did not believe that he was doing anything that was illegal in terms of his Constitutional rights. As he says in Canto 74/426:452: "free speech without free radio speech is as zero." When the Americans landed in Italy, the Italian government collapsed, and the Germans took over the country. Ezra was caught in the capital. After a nightmarish journey from Rome to Gais to see his daughter Mary, he returned to Rapallo and successfully eluded any attempts by Communist guerilas to imprison or kill him.[31] Finally on May 2, 1945, he was apprehended by two bounty-seeking partisans and eventually passed into the hands of the United States Army in Genoa. He was then dispatched to the Disciplinary Training Center (D. T. C.) north of Pisa, where he was incarcerated in an open cage under nightlong lights in the company of murderers and thieves:

> Criminals have no intellectual interests?
> "Hey, Snag, wot are the books ov th' bibl' "
> "name 'em, etc.
> "Latin? I studied latin."
>   said the nigger murderer to his cage-mate.
>   (Canto 76/454:483)

In that improbable place, Pound wrote the *Pisan Cantos*, which many people consider the finest poetry he ever created:

What thou lovest well remains,
              the rest is dross
What thou lov'st well shall not be reft from thee
What thou lov'st well is thy true heritage
                                        (Canto 81/520:556)

After an uncommonly long stretch of imprisonment without trial or formal presentation of charges, he was summarily sent by air to Washington on the night of November 16, 1945, to face death on the charge of treason, largely on the grounds that he had given comfort to the enemy at a time of grave national trouble. He was defended by Julien Cornell, a lawyer appointed by James Laughlin, the owner of New Directions Inc., which had published most of Pound's work after the 1930's.[32] At this dark time he was staunchly defended by many of the people whom he himself had supported in earlier years: Hemingway, Cummings, Eliot, and Marianne Moore. It was felt that the imprisonment had broken the poet to the point where he was incapable of being tried on any charge, and so he was confined to St. Elizabeths Hospital in December. He was thus caught in a frightfully ironic situation where insanity was saving him from charges of treason, and where "regaining his wits" might very well lead to his death.

Despite its obvious horrors, confinement in St. Elizabeths was not without moments of happiness, for the man who had been self-exiled for so many years suddenly found himself back home, surrounded by hundreds of people who had loved his poetry or were simply curious to meet him. Dorothy Pound took up residence in Washington, and she was joined at times by Omar and Mary. In addition, Pound found himself defended by a promising poet named Charles Olson, who was one of the finest craftsmen to perpetuate many of Pound's poetic techniques.

An unfortunate event occurred in 1946 when Bennett Cerf of Random House wanted to delete Pound's poetry from the Modern Library *Anthology of Famous English and American Poetry* edited by William Rose Benét (English section) and Conrad Aiken (American section). Aiken balked, and when the deletion became widely known, Cerf was forced into a humiliating retraction.[33] This controversy was surpassed a few years later when the Fellows in American Letters of the Library of Congress decided to award the Bollingen Prize for poetry to Pound for the publication of the *Pisan Cantos*. The tempest rose to such a pitch that the *Partisan Review*, after some preliminary remarks, devoted space to a symposium of seven contributors, among whom W. H. Auden and Allen Tate, who had been judges, defended the award, and Clement Greenberg and Karl Shapiro attacked it.[34] The vituperation was intensified by Robert Hillyer in an inflamatory article in the *Saturday Review of Literature*, which caused further counterattacks, and although the prize was awarded to Pound, the uproar forced the Library of Congress to withdraw from future aesthetic judgements in favor of Yale University.[35]

Pound continued working, despite his incarceration, publishing his *Rock-Drill Cantos* and the *Confucian Odes (Classical Anthology)* and *Analects*. Finally in April, 1958, largely through the efforts of Archibald MacLeish, Eliot, and a somewhat reluctant Frost, and with a great deal of Italian pressure exerted upon Clare Booth Luce, the American ambassador to Italy and wife of the publisher of *Life* and *Time*, the poet was at last absolved of prosecution (but not cleared of guilt), and remanded into the custody of his wife.

After his release Pound returned to Italy, where he lived at first in Brunnenburg Castle, the home of his daughter Mary. In her book *Discretions*, Mary describes how the situation did not work out; Ezra left not only Brunnenburg but also Dorothy, returning to his lifelong love, Olga Rudge, and residing with her in Sant'Ambrogio or in Venice. He appeared frequently at the Festival of Two Worlds in Spoleto, but otherwise retired gradually from active campaigning for poetry, economics, or politics. Aside from *Thrones* and some fragments, his last major publication was his richly original translation of Sophocles' *Women of Trachis*, which appeared in book form in London in 1956.

Pound died in Venice on November 1, 1972, two days after his eighty-seventh birthday. He was buried in the island cemetery of San Michele after a simple, sparsely attended funeral that did not include Dorothy or Omar, and that attracted no official notice from the Italian or American governments. Before his death, all who met Pound commented on his uniquely grand appearance, which he maintained into old age. But now he was also given to long periods of deep silence.[36] Gone were the frenzy and furor of the past, except for brief snatches in *Thrones*. As he himself said in a beautiful line from Canto 83/529:564: "the sage/delighteth in water." In his old age, the son of Scorpio had at last learned tranquility.

As we have seen in unraveling the stories of the two men's lives, there are many striking similarities. Not the least of these is a likeness in temperament, for the Italian was often as aggressive, tactless, impassioned, and full of crusading zeal as his American counterpart. Aside from the temperament shown in his letters, Dante was described as follows by the usually fair-minded Giovanni Villani, who lived at a time when he was able to make a just assessment:

> This Dante, because of his knowledge, was somewhat arrogant and withdrawn and disdainful, and after the manner of a philosopher, heedless of graces and not relaxed in his conversation with laymen.
>
> *(Cronica,* IX.136)

The description sounds strangely like many made by the various people who knew Pound in his Paris and London days. Furthermore, to show that Dante was not greeted with the same ease that twentieth-century critics tend to show to him, Villani notes in the same passage: "It is true that in his *Comedy* he liked to denounce and rail out in the manner of poets, perhaps in certain places more than he should have." Need one say more?

In short, a man who is going to undertake to judge his own age and all of the centuries of the past is one who must of necessity be somewhere between a prophet and a madman—depending on whether you are Pope Boniface or Henry VII judging Dante, or Roosevelt or Il Duce assessing Pound. When one starts to judge judgements, he suddenly realizes the enormous relativity of positions—a thing that neither Dante nor Pound, in creating them, can grant. Yet this task, which is thrust upon the reader, is probably the best reason for reading such works. One is forced into thought.

The writer of any epic is forced to take a stand, and both authors are far removed from the positions of the establishments of their day. Vergil seems to have toadied to Augustus, and Milton was apparently content to be the official spokesman for Puritanism, but neither Dante nor Pound will become an apologist for his time; they are too critical, and, in a sense, too progressive.

Both Dante and Pound seem to have been primarily impelled to write their epics because they keenly felt that they themselves had

been judged: Dante by the Florentine Blacks and the Papacy; Pound
by the Protestant trustees of Wabash College, the Midwest ethos, or,
in broader terms, the America of the first decade of this century. In
Dante's case the exile was thrust upon him through contrived
charges. In Pound's case, the exile was undertaken ostensibly at his
own decision. However, if we examine the lives of many of the major
writers of this century—James, Eliot, Hemingway, Stein—do we not
learn that expatriation was almost a form of exile, that every artist felt
that his exclusion had been thrust upon him by a material, Philistine
society that was utterly inimical?

Pound, in fact, had to suffer exile again and again:

> so that leaving America I brought with me $80
> and England a letter of Thomas Hardy's
> and Italy one eucalyptus pip
> from the salita that goes up from Rapallo.

(Canto 80/500:533)

The exile from America was simply the first (a departure with cold
hard cash, the chief American export of the day); the English banishment came with literature, which he had hoped to find there; the
Italian banishment, which was really a recall to his native land, took
place with a loose bit of nature in his hand. Pound's true dark night of
the soul (*atra nox animae*) was every bit as horrible and humiliating as
Dante's. The fact that America forgave him in a reasonable way that
Pound could accept, as Florence never did to Dante, did not ultimately make things easier. On attaining freedom, Pound left his
native land once again for his beloved Italy.

Looking at both lives, we can see a strong similarity in the two
men's intellectual developments. Both began as lyric poets, but soon
moved on to philosophical themes with strong political implications.
In Dante's case, we are told that the death of Beatrice drove him to
philosophy and that the exile from Florence impelled him headlong
into international politics. In Pound's case we surmise that the pov-
erty of his brilliant friends in the London after World War I, as well as
the horrors of the war itself, were the chief factors leading him from
aesthetics to more empirical pursuits.

There is no doubt that both epics fall into the general patterns of
the poets' lives. As was pointed out with Dante, the *Inferno* was
undoubtedly written in the years shortly after the exile itself, when
the poet was truly wandering in a dark valley of despair. His

Purgatorio probably was composed in that optimistic part of his life which saw the rising role of Imperial Germany in Italy. His *Paradiso* was probably composed for the most part in the last phase of his career, when the old man had turned his eyes away from any Earthly Messiah and was working toward his private vision of the light. The movement thus proceeds from suffering through striving to illumination. It is, in fact, the classical tragic rhythm that forms a strange contrasting frame for the "comic" vision of the epic itself. The pilgrim Dante within the poem enjoys a complete vision of the universe from dissolution to fulfillment. The writer Dante follows the divergent path of the tragic seer.

The same kind of gap can be seen between Pound's life and work. The earlier *Cantos* containing many disruptive visions were composed after the World War I period, largely in England. The middle cantos, which present vast sections dealing with the happy societies of China and America, were written during the golden days of the Mussolini period. The last cantos, which are often visionary, were composed after the cathartic experiences of the Pisan Detention Camp and the insane asylum in Washington. Pound, even more than Dante, lived his life through his work.

Both poets in their dynamic searches for the truth abandon the apparently easy road of the traditional epic poet, who is happy to hymn his native land, no matter what it does. Both embark on that far lonelier road that Oedipus took to Colonus, the journey of a man who has witnessed all and whose final role can only be one of silence.

2

LYRIC YOUTH: PRECISION AND PERSONAE

In the previous chapter we noted that both of these writers of epic began their careers as lyric poets. Undoubtedly this youthful preoccupation had some effect upon their later work, both with respect to their treatment of the individual word and to their concept of the epic poem as a complex of lyrics. In examining Dante we shall try to trace out the principles which underlie his work. In moving to Pound, we will see if these principles are perpetuated and if so, how.

Let us begin by identifying the prime influences on the Italian. Dante lets us know frankly that his primary source for the art of poetry was Vergil. He addresses the Roman thus when he first sees him:

> "Are you that Vergil, then? Are you the fount
> that issues such a mighty river of speech?"
> I answered him with a shamefilled front.
> "O honor and light of all the other poets,
> may that long study and that steady love
> that made me search your volume avail me now!
> You are my only master, my sole author;
> you are alone the one from whom I snatched
> the beautiful style that has won me honor."
>
> (*Inf.* 1.79 ff.)

We may notice that Dante is not thanking Vergil for philosophical assistance; he is praising him entirely in terms of rhetoric, the *bello stile* that he had already perfected in 1300, the year of the vision of the *Comedy*.

What did Vergil specifically teach the Italian? This is an interesting question because it points up a strong contrast with Pound, who abhorred Vergil for being an inflated word-colorer and a starry-eyed romantic.[1] Dante probably meant exactly what he said, that he admired the entire corpus line by line. But unquestionably such gems as *Eclogues* IV and X must have stood out in his mind, just as they did in the minds of other medieval writers.[2] Indeed, since Dante probably did not know Greek to any extent,[3] who else could have wielded a stronger influence from the past? Actually in *Inferno* IV.70 ff., Dante does add a few more names:

> We were still a little way off from there
> but not so much that I couldn't in part discern
> that an honorable people possessed that place.
> "O you who honor the sciences and arts,
> who are these men who have such mighty honor
> that their style of life sets them so apart?"
> And he to me: "The honor of their names
> that vibrates from them upward into your life
> acquires for them a grace that advances them."
> And suddenly a voice was heard by me:
> "All give honor to the highest poet!
> His shade's returning now that went away."
> After that voice was rested and was quiet
> I saw four great shadows coming toward us
> bearing a look that was neither glad nor sad.
> My good master then began to speak:
> "Look at that man holding the sword in hand,
> who comes ahead of the other three as lord.
> That one is Homer, poet sovereign.
> The second is Horace the satirist who comes;
> Ovid is third; the last of them is Lucan."

We cannot fail to notice how the word "honor" resounds in this passage. It occurs in some form eight times in the entire canto.[4] Here, then, is Dante's pantheon: Vergil, Homer, Horace, Ovid, and Lucan. The last-named may surprise the modern reader, but Dante admired such passages as the description of the snakes in the *Pharsalia*, which he put to use in *Inferno* XXIV and XXV.[5] Pound would approve of the others, with perhaps a grudging nod toward Horace, a poet whom he admired for little more than metrical virtuosity.[6] These five writers are also mentioned in the *Vita Nuova*, Chapter XXV, thus re-enforcing their importance to the Italian. Homer could be grasped even without Greek through Vergil. Ovid's presence is not felt as strongly with Dante as it is with Pound, but Ezra insisted on that poet's influence on Alighieri.[7]

We must now consider contemporary influences. It is safe to say that, aside from the other members of the *dolce stil nuovo*, the poets who had the most important effect on Dante were the troubadours. If we put one of the early *Vita Nuova* lyrics like *Morte villana* of Chapter VIII next to a song of Arnaut Daniel's that Dante praises in the *De vulgari* (II.6), we can see the important differences that define the achievement of the *dolce stil nuovo*.[8] The Dante poem, printed by Pound in *The Spirit of Romance* in the translation of Rossetti, runs as follows:

> Death, always cruel, Pity's foe in chief,
> Mother who brought forth grief,
> Merciless judgment and without appeal!
> Since thou alone hast made my heart to feel
> This sadness and unweal,
> My tongue upbraideth thee without relief.[9]

The Arnaut poem in Pound's translation from the same volume (p. 26) reads:

> Only I know what over-anguish falls
> Upon the love-worn heart through over-love.
> Because of my desire so firm and whole
> Toward her I loved on sight and since alway,
> Which turneth not aside nor wavereth.
> So, far from her, I speak for her mad speech,
> Who near her, for o'er much to speak, am dumb.

The basic differences are obvious: the Italian lyric is somber and serious; the Provençal poem is light and playful.[10] As I said in *Seven Troubadours*, the key word in Provençal is *joi*, "joy."[11] Pound himself described these differences when he said: "The Provençal canzone can be understood when sung. Tuscan canzoni often require close study in print before they will yield their meaning" (*Spirit*, p. 113). Formally the troubadours also differ from Dante and the Italians in one major respect: the troubadour *cansos* tend to be loose, irrationally joined, not moving in any special direction. Dante's lyric poetry, as Erich Auerbach has demonstrated, is concise, logically ordered, and constantly moving toward an end.[12] The Italian de-

velopment of the sonnet, the tightly organized fourteen-liner, contrasts sharply with the leisurely Provençal *canso*.[13]
We might now move to the famous passage in the *Purgatorio* XXIV.49 ff. to find out what Dante himself has to say about the "sweet new style" that he helped to create with Cavalcanti, Lapo Gianni, Cino of Pistoia, and others.[14] The speaker here is Bonagiunta of Lucca, a poet of an older school who is suffering in the round of Gluttons:

> "But tell me, do I see here the man
> who drew forth that new poem that begins
> *Ladies who have intellect of love?*"
> And I to him: "I am the kind of man who,
> once Love breathes on me, takes note, and in the mode
> he dictates (*ditta*) in me, I go forth making meanings."
> "O brother, now I see," said he, "the knot
> that held back the Notary, Guittone, and me
> from gaining that sweet new style that I hear."

The lines are open to many different interpretations, but a few basic points can be established.[15] Bonagiunta has singled out for praise the famous *Donne ch'avete intelletto d'amore* of *Vita Nuova* XIX, and Dante replies that the work was written in the following way: 1) under the direct impact of Love; 2) with inspiration: the "breathes on me" (*mi spira*) suggests direct inspiring; 3) in an incontrovertible way ("dictates in me") that is opposed to romantic looseness; 4) in a serious philosophical sense ("making meanings," *significando*), not in the playful rhetorical style typical of Bonagiunta and his peers, Guittone d'Arezzo and the Notary Giacomo da Lentino.[16] If, on the other hand, we take a look at one of the Cavalcanti translations done by Pound, we can quickly spot the tone, the form, and the diction that are characteristic of Dante's early work.[17]

One can connect Dante with the troubadors only in terms of the content of the early parts of the *Vita Nuova*, where love is depicted as a sensual, irrational upheaval. Later, it is approached philosophically. Pound put his finger on the difference when he said in *The Spirit of Romance* (p. 116): "The cult of Provence had been a cult of the emotions; and with it there had been some, hardly conscious, study of emotional psychology. In Tuscany the cult is a cult of the harmonies of the mind." Pound the youthful critic was a skilled observer of the youthful poet Dante.

Alighieri's violent dislike of Guittone d'Arezzo was repeated in
Purgatorio XXVI.115 ff. by Guido Guinizelli, whom Dante names as
his philosophical authority in *Vita Nuova* XX:

> "O my brother," said he, "that one I'm pointing out
> with my finger," and he pointed to a spirit up ahead,
> "*he* was a better craftsman of our mother tongue.
> Verses of love and proses of romance
> he outstripped far. And let the fools contend
> that that one from Limoges is in the forefront.
> They turn their faces more to rumor than truth,
> and thus they seal their opinions closed
> before either art or reason can be heard.
> That's the way the men of old treated Guittone,
> giving him praise, heaping cry upon cry,
> but now the truth has vanquished him with most."

The words that strike one in this passage are "better craftsman"
(miglior fabbro). It is obvious that Dante, like Pound and Eliot (who
used this very phrase as his dedication of *The Waste Land* to Ezra),
thought of the poet as an artisan. This emphasis upon precision
became almost synonymous with Pound's name, since he brought
Catullan crispness, haiku clarity, and Flaubertian striving for the *mot
juste* together in his imagistic manifestos.

The most troublesome word in Dante's aesthetic canon is
"sweet." But here the treatise *De vulgari eloquentia* is a help. In Part
II, Chapters 6 and 7, Dante speaks of the various ascending styles of
rhetoric. The range extends in words from the lowly *mamma*, which
he himself employs in *Purgatorio* XXX.44 f., to the lordly trisyllabic
amore or *disio*, fundamental words in love poetry. In complete sen-
tences, the lowly or mundane (Latin *insipidus*) style is exemplified by
Petrus amat multum dominam Bertam, "Peter loves Lady Bertha
very much." Moving upward, Dante settles on this example of a
sentence that is light, high-sounding, and *sapidus* (full of good flavor):
*Eiecta maxima parte florum de sinu tuo, Florentia, nequicquam
Trinacriam Totila secundus adivit*, "Having chased away the greater
part of the flowers from your bosom, O Florence, in vain did Totila
the Second go away to Sicily." The translation may sound artificial,
but in the original Latin we can see what Dante is driving toward: he is
trying to combine a metaphoric statement that is contained in
"flowers from your bosom" with plain, direct words like *eiecta* and

adivit. There is a discernible musical lilt to the whole, beginning with the suspenseful initial ablative absolute and moving past the gentle echo of *florum* in *Florentia,* past the dental alliterations, and finally culminating in the unadorned but forceful stop-word *adivit.* In short, the sentence shows the expression of a concept in a balance between rhetorical flourish and direct statement. It combines art with simplicity in a way that agrees with the essence of Pound's aesthetic philosophy as expressed in the *ABC of Reading.*

Dante goes on to cite some poets who have managed to blend poetic techniques with the direct conciseness of prose, naming Arnaut Daniel, Guinizelli, Cavalcanti, Cino of Pistoia, and himself for his *Amor che ne la mente mi ragiona* of *Convivio* III. He recommends that people study Vergil, Ovid's *Metamorphoses,* Statius, and Lucan among poets, as well as Livy, Pliny, Frontinus, and Paulus Orosius among prose writers. Finally he ends with still another condemnation of Guittone and his ilk for what Dante terms *plebescere,* "being common." By now we must conclude that the cardinal sins of poetic composition are artificial rhetoric and cheap, mundane rhetoric. If, in fact, we take a look at Dante's nemesis, we find that Guittone fluctuates between two extremes: hollow, wooden artifice such as was typical of the worst of the earlier Sicilian School, and, on the other side, a loose, imprecise, perennially abstract kind of diction that suggests an attempt to imitate the voice of the people, but merely mimics a jaded form of prose.[18] These two extremes are clearly what Dante was warning the prospective writer against. In his own day Pound inveighed against similar vices: on one hand, the false artifice of Rupert Brooke, Tennyson, and the then fashionable Victorians and Edwardians; and on the other the false folksiness of Vachel Lindsay, Frost in his later phases, and Sandburg at his crudest. Although Dante always shows great respect for the fully blown rhetorical style, the so-called "tragic" style of the *Aeneid,* when he came to forge his mighty epos, he stayed with the language of the people. As Cavalcanti had suggested, he ultimately chose the comic or mixed style over the highly elevated. Similarly Pound in his mature writing of the *Cantos* blends his styles from the folksy, cracker-barrel phraseology of Uncle Ez to the most refined poetry about Neoplatonic light.[19] Both writers believed in the joy of differing textures.

Returning to the *Vita Nuova,* we can see the aesthetic principles of the later *De vulgari* already put into use. Throughout the account of his early life Dante selects the proper word with care. For example, he goes so far as to print two openings for the sonnet in Chapter XXXIV. He distinguishes between a palmer and a pilgrim meaningfully in Chapter XL. He puns and weaves allegorical meanings out of names in Chapter XXIV. Everywhere he shows himself as a craftsman of words, but in no place is this skill more evident than in the attitude he adopts toward his own poems. Some scholars have considered these commentaries travesties; others have tried to interpret them in a biblical-exegetical way, as if Dante were posing as a kind of St. Thomas Aquinas analyzing his own work.[20] I would not overrule this last interpretation, but I believe that Dante analyzed his poetry largely for aesthetic reasons, to show how carefully, how thoughtfully the forms were worked out. In this way he writes off romantic theories of composition just as Pound was to do later. Granted that his analyses really tell us little; we must remember that Dante is concerned primarily with methodology. When Vergil appears hoarse in *Inferno* I.63, Dante is trying to tell us allegorically that the art of poetry in his day is weak. We know from the mention of Cavalcanti in *Vita Nuova* XXV that most of the masses, and especially the women, were ignorant of Latin. As a result, Dante explicates, just as Pound was to do in "How to Read" and in the *ABC of Reading*. Both also make the Greco-Roman classics the center of their curriculum. Educating the reader was in some ways as important to both men as exercising the craft of poet.

Aside from its refined precision, the *Vita Nuova* also contains dramatic realism. Although many scholars like Singleton and Shaw choose to accentuate the mystical, hieratic nature of the work—and no one will argue its presence—still one must agree with Francesco de Sanctis that Beatrice and the work itself are fusions of the ideals of troubadours, Christians, and philosophers.[21] The *Vita Nuova* blends esoteric mysticism with a quite realistic account of the agon of love. Most importantly, the poems in the book rise out of the poet's history. They are not conjured up out of a void, as are so many of the poems of the Sicilian School; nor are they dredged from a store of clichés, as so much of Petrarch sounded to Pound.

Looking at the framework, we see that the very first poem describes a terrifying vision that Dante had of his beloved lying half-nude in the arms of Love, who forces her to eat the heart of the poet and then carries her off into the heavens. Although this work may seem to be the product of a young man's romantic dreams, everyone ignores the fantastic element and drives toward the poem's philosophic import. When Cavalcanti answers Dante in an explicatory poem (translated by Pound "Thou sawest, it seems to me, all things availing"; *Trans.*, p. 69), in which he believes that Dante's dream is a marvelous vision of cosmic splendor, Dante does not buy the grand reply. He clings to the desperate details of the poem and remarks, rather cryptically, that the dream was a true prelude of future events. We may conclude that the fantastic elements of the poem determine the actual elements of the plot, and indeed this is what happens: Beatrice devours the poet's heart and ascends into the heavens. What seems mere fictive idling is in actuality a precursor to a metaphysical vision. In fact, the prose sections of the *Vita Nuova* are there primarily to lend substance to a sequence of poems that might have otherwise seemed mystifying or unreal. Dante uses prose for a utilitarian purpose in a way that is as direct as that of Flaubert.[22] Many of his poems begin with lines that contain the unfolding of a dramatic moment: "Villainous death, enemy of mercy" (VIII); "Riding the other day upon a highway" (IX); "My lady carries Love within her eyes" (XXI); "You who bear a humble look" (XXII); "Alas, pilgrims, who go so thoughtfully" (XL). By comparison even the skilled Cavalcanti and Guinizelli sometimes sound abstract.

If one takes a long poem like the previously cited "Ladies who have intellect of love," he cannot help but notice the way that that work progresses with impressive logic from the manifesto-sounding call of the opening invocation to a portrayal of Heaven, which is demanding Beatrice among its ranks. The structure of the canzone shows how Dante was capable of using the dramatic voice for achieving variety in the poem's texture. Dante addresses the ladies in stanza one; an angel talks in stanza two, where Pity stands up for the poet; Dante re-addresses the ladies in stanza three; Love discourses on Beatrice's great powers in stanza four; Dante talks to the song itself in stanza five, sending it on its way. Never does a Provençal *canso* show such an intricate, shifting mode of organization.

In such poems Dante is defeating the stifling, ego-centered voice that wails monotonously in the decadent Provençal love song. Similarly Pound in a later age donned masks as a means of avoiding the self-conscious, self-pitying tone of much of Victorian poetry.[23] One feels in Dante's hands a lyric becoming more than a lyric, becoming in fact at times a dramatic dialogue. The implications of this are important, for in many ways Dante's epic is a symphony of voices or, as Pound put it in *The Spirit of Romance* (p. 154): "a great mystery play, or better, a cycle of mystery plays." It is never, at any rate, the consistent expression of a simplistic lyric sensibility, as faulty epic can sometimes be.[24]

If we take the very epigrammatic sonnet of *Vita Nuova* XX and set it beside the famous Guinizelli poem, *Al cor gentil rempaira sempre amore* ("Love always repairs to the gentle or noble heart"), we can see the effective way in which Dante reduces the complex but repetitious poem of Guinzelli to simpler, more dramatic terms.[25] Both poems make the same general statement: Love and nobility cannot exist without each other; and both use precise metaphors to convey their ideas. The difference is that Guinizelli does it again and again with a series of cosmic correspondences (the sun and the mud, the star or magnetic influence and the stone, the heat and the fire), whereas Dante restricts his references to a single place, the heart, with personifications to enliven the detail. Dante is more compressed than his rival. He shows a gift for condensation, a term that Pound quite correctly conceived as the heart of the poetic process.[26]

We might now generalize and say that Dante's early aesthetic philosophy (even though much was expressed in the later *De vulgari*) was based on two broad principles: 1) precision in words and images; and 2) dramatic presentation of characters and events, including the mediating voice of a poem. Dante shows a complete awareness of critical ideas as a youthful poet, and Pound, as a youthful critic, soon demonstrated his own appreciation for his forerunner. As early as *The Spirit of Romance*, Pound said: "Dante's precision both in the *Vita Nuova* and in the *Commedia* comes from the attempt to reproduce exactly the thing which has been clearly seen" (p. 126). Later in the *ABC of Reading* he added: "You have to go almost exclusively to Dante's criticism to find a set of OBJECTIVE categories for words" (p. 37). In fact, in his first very important book of criticism, *Spirit*, Pound used Dante almost exclusively in discussing the troubadours in the second and third chapters. Following Alighieri, Pound allowed Arnaut Daniel to emerge as the chief singer of Provençal, even though most modern Provençalists such as T. G. Bergin tend to find that man's virtuosity a bit excessive.[27] Pound, however, insisted on see-

ing the two poets as members of a kindred cause, as when he said of
Dante in *Spirit* (p. 159):

> His vividness depends much on his comparison by simile to particular
> phenomena; this we have already noted in the chapter on Arnaut Daniel; thus
> Dante, following the Provençal, says, not "where a river pools itself," but "As
> at Arles, where the Rhone pools itself."

When he cites a brilliant simile from *Paradiso* XXVI.85, Pound gives
Arnaut some credit for the type of presentation (p. 150). We know, of
course, from the fact that Dante bestowed the rare privilege of allow-
ing Arnaut to speak in Provençal in *Purgatorio* XXVI, that Dante
admired the troubadour quite genuinely, but Pound's adulation of
Arnaut goes far beyond that.

One could easily say that the outline of *The Spirit of Romance* is
dictated by the guidelines established by Dante: beginning with the
Latin classics and ending with the decline of literature after the *dolce
stil nuovo*. What Pound calls "the spirit of romance" is actually the
pagan current typified by Ovid running below the surface of the
Middle Ages and coming up again in the Renaissance. It is a brook of
clarity, according to Pound, that Christianity tried to stop in its
striving for the total life of the spirit; but a troubadour like Arnaut
Daniel kept the song of the birds alive, kept the cult of Natura
flourishing, in the very sounds or *melopoeia* he created:

> *L'aura amara*
> *Fals bruoills brancutz*
> *Clarzir*
> *Quel doutz espeissa ab fuoills,*
> *Els letz*
> *Becs*
> *Dels auzels ramencs*
> *Ten balps e mutz*
> *Pars*
> *E non-pars.*[28]

Arnaut is like Clement Janequin, whose bird-imitative music appears
transcribed in Canto 75. He is a man who, in the translated terminology of Erich Auerbach, contended against the "vulgar spiritualism"
of his age.[29] Pound sees both Dante and Cavalcanti as continuers of
this tradition, who added something in the form of philosophy; but
Pound would be very much in agreement with the subtitle of one of

Auerbach's early books, when the scholar called Dante a "poet of the secular world."
Dante's significance to Pound extended far beyond rhetoric. Ezra included the Italian when he was establishing his guideposts for an ideal education in "How to Read" (*Essays*, p. 38): Confucius, Homer, Ovid, Provençal Song Book ("With cross reference to Minnesingers, and to Bion, perhaps thirty poems in all"), Dante ("And his circle"), Villon, and then he jumped to Voltaire and the nineteenth century. Later, in an addendum to his *Guide to Kulchur* Pound established the following seven focal points in the section called "As Sextant" (p. 352):

I. The FOUR BOOKS (Confucius and Mencius).
II. HOMER: Odyssey: intelligence set above brute force.
III. The Greek TRAGEDIANS: rise of sense of civic responsibility.
IV. DIVINA COMMEDIA: life of the spirit.
V. FROBENIUS: Erlebte Erdteile . . .
V.I. BROOKS ADAMS . . .
VII. The English Charters, the essential parts of BLACKSTONE . . . The American Constitution.

If any further evidence of Dante's importance were needed, one would only have to turn to Pound's words to René Taupin (*Letters*, pp. 216 ff.) or to Laurence Binyon (pp. 251 ff.).

There is also no doubt that Dante must be counted as a force in Pound's ideas about imagism. In the famous letter written in 1915 to Harriet Monroe, in which Pound said "Poetry must be *as well written as prose*," Ezra lays down the laws in precisely the same terms he used to describe Dante's own writings in *Spirit:* "Objectivity and again objectivity, and expression"; "Language is made out of concrete things" (*Letters*, pp. 48 f.). All of the Dantesque ideas were brought to a focus when Pound issued the three primary dicta for imagism, published first in *Poetry* in 1913 and reprinted in many forms (*Essays*, pp. 3 ff.):

1. Direct treatment of the "thing" . . .
2. . . . no word that does not contribute to the presentation.
3. . . . compose in the sequence of the musical phrase, not in the sequence of a metronome.

Yet it is to Pound's poetry, rather than to his letters and criticism, that one should go to see the Dantesque ideas put into act. In the 1965 reprint of Pound's first book of published poems, *A Lume Spento,* we can see an attempt to blend various shades of language according to Dantesque prescriptions. As Pound showed in the *ABC of Reading* (p. 37), he was well aware of the fact that Dante "called words 'buttered' and 'shaggy' because of the different NOISES they make. Or *pexta et hirsuta,* combed and hairy." One of the primary samples of Dante's own blending of styles occurs in *Paradiso* XVII.129, when he has Cacciaguida utter a very "shaggy" line: "And let them scratch where they feel the itch" (*e lascia pur grattar dov'è la rogna*). A similarly bold use of language occurs in much of Pound's earliest writing:

> Heart that was big as the bowels of Vesuvius
> ("Mesmerism," *A Lume Spento,* 1965 ed., p. 28)

> 'Pollo Phoibee, to our way-fare
> Make thy laugh our wander-lied. . .
> Seeking e'er the new-laid rast-way
> To the gardens of the sun. . .
> ("Cino," ibid., p. 18)

A daring mixture of tenderness and toughness that is typical of Dante is beautifully conveyed throughout "A Villonaud: Ballad of the Gibbet," especially in the following lines on page 27:

> Skoal!! to the gallows! and then pray we:
> God damn his hell out speedily
> And bring their souls to his "Haulte Citee."

In this case, Villon, as the title indicates, is probably as much to be credited as Dante. But both Villon and Dante offered Pound samples of the kind of masculine rhetoric that was necessary to expel the effeminate sighs of late Victorian verse.

Some of the poems in *A Lume Spento* were clearly inferior, and were omitted from the *Personae: Collected Poems* of 1926 and subsequent years. It is perhaps unfair to look at these, but they do help us to gauge the progress that Pound made in his youth. "A Rouse," which attempts to catch the pagan flavor of a Provençal alba, contains the following mixed-bag as a final strophe (p. 77):

> Breath of mirth,
> My bed, my bower green of earth,

Naught else hath any worth.
Save ye, "jolif bachillier"!
Hell take the hin'most!

Similarly the poem "Nicotine: A Hymn to the Dope" (pp. 78 f.)
shows a wobbly sense of diction. In the title alone, the word
"nicotine" is too technical in the wrong way and "dope" is too
slangy.
   Other poems in *A Lume Spento* give indications of the accomplished poetry that was to follow. The elegant, measured tones of the
lyrical Dante and Cavalcanti can be heard in a poem like "Donzella
Beata" (p. 41).[30] One of the loveliest poems, "In Epitaphium Eius"
(p. 20), concerns a troubadour who was called

      . . . fickle that the lambent flame
Caught "Bicé" dreaming in each new-blown name,

And loved all fairness though its hidden guise
Lurked various in half an hundred eyes;

That loved the essence though each casement bore
A different semblance than the one before.

Here Bertran de Born, who created his Song for the Self-Conceived
Lady,[31] seems to be merged with Dante, or should we say that all
idealizing poets are merged into the one voice of the Seeker for
Beauty, and the woman, loosely called Bicé (short for Beatrice), is a
symbol of the thing searched for.
   As he shows in "Masks" (p. 52), Pound was already aware that
to create lasting objects of beauty he would have to move outside of
himself in the London Hell and don the masks of the past. Whether he
learned this technique from Browning or from the many voices of the
Divine Comedy is not worth debating here. He was aware of this
necessity in the long letter he wrote to William Carlos Williams on
October 21, 1908, from London, answering Williams' objections to
the pessimistic and dissolute qualities of the work: "Remember, of
course, that some of the stuff is dramatic and in the character of the
person named in the title" (*Letters*, p. 3). This concept of the lyric as a
dramatic vehicle was as essential to Pound as it was to Dante. And it is
perhaps inevitable that Pound, steeped in Dante, should even toy
with the idea of assuming the Italian's mask. We can see some playful

hinting of this in the poem "Histrion," which was first published in 1908 in *A Quinzaine for This Yule* and was reprinted in the 1965 edition of *A Lume Spento* (p. 108):

> No man hath dared to write this thing as yet,
> And yet I know, how that the souls of all men great
> At times pass through us,
> And we are melted into them, and are not
> Save reflexions of their souls.
> Thus am I Dante for a space and am
> One François Villon, ballad-lord and thief,
> Or am such holy ones I may not write
> Lest blasphemy be writ against my name.

This process of assuming the voice of Dante was made even more complete in the poem "Scriptor Ignotus" (*A Lume Spento,* 1965 ed., pp. 38 ff.), which is dedicated to the pianist Katherine Ruth Heyman through the initials K. R. H. This poem shows the unique way in which Pound was able to blend his voices in a subtle manner. Bearing the dateline "Ferrara 1715," the lyric contains a note at the end which tells the reader that it is written in the person of "Bertold Lomax, English Dante scholar and mystic" who "died in Ferrara in 1723, with his 'great epic' still a mere shadow, a nebula crossed with some few gleams of wonder light. The lady of the poem was an organist of Ferrara, whose memory has come down to us only in Lomax's notes."

In this poem Lomax, the narrator, who has Pound behind him, addresses his nameless lady, telling her that he, like the Dante of the *Vita Nuova,* will strive to do something for her that will make her earthly glory even greater. The narrator claims that he will

> . . . make for thee and for the beauty of thy music
> A new thing
> As hath not heretofore been writ.

Earlier he speaks of "that great forty-year epic/ That you know of, yet unwrit." In this poem Pound indicates the enormity of his debt to Dante, both future and present. The debt goes beyond meter, words, and form. It extends from the very matrix of Pound's early beliefs, as expressed in his philosophy of imagism and his use of dramatic personas, into the poet's life purpose and aim. This poem shows that

Pound, in assuming the voice of Lomax, was really searching for the voice and role of Dante. The young Pound had found the young Dante essential in forming ideas of criticism that would dominate his future compositions. But the young Pound was also haunted by the dream of a man who could embark on the writing of a long poem in honor of his lady, a poem that would in effect encompass the world in which he and the lady lived, and also all that was known of the world up until that time. In the next chapter, we shall discuss the ways in which both poets turned from the lyrical creativity of youth to the epic pursuits that occupied the most important parts of their lifetimes.

3

THE QUEST FOR AIM

The bays that formerly old Dante crowned
Are worn today by Ezra Loomis Pound.
PUNCH (January 22, 1913)

There is a kind of poet who seems to have some sense of his entire career at an early age, and whose development is simply a filling in of detail. Such a writer was James Joyce, whose *Dubliners*, *Ulysses*, and *Finnegans Wake* move in centrifugal patterns ever outward from the realistic details of Dublin into the archetypal patterns of human unconsciousness.[1] Both Dante and Pound always seem to have had some sense of where they were going, even if their paths do not run in direct lines. In the poem cited at the close of Chapter 2, Pound announced through the voice of Lomax his intention to write The Great Modern Epic. Similarly at the end of the *Vita Nuova* Dante declared his intention to write "something of her that was never written of any other woman." But in neither case did the fulfillment follow as smoothly as the announcement of the intention. Between the book of Dante's youth and the comedy of his maturity lie several scattered rhymes, two specialized treatises, and that puzzling work that is called the *Convivio* or *Convito*, "The Banquet."

This work has always been something of a problem for any but the most confirmed Dantistas. The German scholar Karl Vossler referred to it as a "labored" and "tasteless" exercise in "philosophic dilettantism."[2] Pound, though sympathetic, gives it relatively short treatment in *The Spirit of Romance*, Chapter 6, although he does refer to the tireless beauty of the first poem of the work, and seems to admire the philosophical structure that underlies most of the poetry. In the final *Cantos*, he shows his full appreciation of the work by using it extensively to support his own ideas about philosophy.

The fact is that the *Convivio* is more of an interruption in Dante's career than a direct link in a linear development. The reason is simple: the *Vita Nuova* had sung of the passion of love in a way that Dante calls in *Convivio* I.i.17 "fervent and passionate," in an almost feminine or passive sense. Here Dante was largely acted upon, thrown down into the pitfalls of *dianoia* (senses), the lowest portion of the Christian Neoplatonic scheme as developed by one of Pound's favorite philosophers, Scotus Erigena.[3] Now in his second major work, Dante attempts something new, something *"temperata e virile"* (tempered, balanced, manly; I.i.17). We can say that this attempt consists of a movement upward into the second realm of Logos or Reason if we adhere to the Erigenistic corporal microcosm for our basic structure.[4] Or, to put it in Dante's own words, as he comments at the end of his discussion of *Voi che 'ntendendo*, he will hymn the praise of Lady Philosophy (II.xv), just as before he had hymned the praise of Beatrice. As a result, Dante has dismissed the guiding genius of his early work, and has adopted a new lady. Since we know what Beatrice stands for in the later *Comedy*, we can see allegorically that Dante has put aside Godly Beatitude and has followed instead in the steps of Human Wisdom. Even someone without a vestige of medieval lore could guess the outcome of this change. The *Convivio* offers us only three poems out of a projected fourteen, and the scheme is then abandoned. The reason is apparent: lack of aim, lack of form, lack of a scaffolding upon which to hang his accomplished and obscure poetry in a way that would make sense to himself and his audience.

The *Convivio* does not trail off the way the *De vulgari* does, where the poet seems to have exhausted the major things that interested him (metrics, diction, the history of language) and to have descended into things too small for his notice (elegiac and comic modes of poetizing). The *Convivio* simply pulls to a halt as if the poet had suddenly realized that he had come from nowhere and was going in the same direction. He was, to take the metaphor of *Inferno* I, "lost in a darkened wood." Dante needed illumination, direction, aim.

Almost in answer to this need he sees the luminous rays of the Sun in *Inferno* I and encounters the commanding figure of Vergil. This miraculous event was inspired, he is told, by the descent of Beatrice from the outer stretches of the Universe into the dark center of matter, to propel the kind, paternal figure of the Roman poet to lead her lost man onto a straightened path. In allegorical terms, Divine Grace enters Evil Matter to summon Human Reason to lead Man on his quest for salvation. Crude as this spelling out may be, it nevertheless clarifies the poles of Dante's thought.

To return to the tripartite Erigenistic concept of macrocosm and human microcosm, Dante had to discover the third and uppermost level: Nous, Mind, Spirit in its highest, most intellectual sense. This is what imbues the whole man; this is what enables the complete poet to sing of the pain of tactile things, the life of the senses in the *Inferno*, to pursue virtue through the good deeds of human activity in the *Purgatorio*, and to enter that final ineffable realm of the *Paradiso*, where communication is best conveyed through form, symbol, and a gathering of light. This miraculous wholeness, which many medieval thinkers would simply call Soul—the "entelechy or total form of a being having life," as Aristotle expressed it in the opening of his *De Anima*—is a thing that sings, a thing that can be heard in the rhapsodic opening verses of the *Comedy* in a way that the dry, intellectual verses of the *Convivio* never attain, weighted as they are with self-conscious, rather pompous commentaries.

In summary, we might say that in writing the *Comedy*, Dante found two things: 1) Beatrice, whom he had lost after the *Vita Nuova;* and 2) Vergil, whose own sense of the founding of Rome, the Eternal Earthly City, was backed by his knowledge of the Underworld, a place where eternal values existed, if only in a negative way. The female figure represents guiding idealism; the male, probing realism. Both are important, and neither was truly present in the *Convivio*.

The loss of Beatrice is unquestionably cataclysmic for Dante during this middle period of his life. She herself states it in harsh terms in *Purgatorio* XXX.31, when she appears in mighty triumph while beloved Vergil fades away in the shadows:

Above veiled in white girt by olive
a lady appeared to me, under a mantle of green,
clothed in the color of a living flame.
And my spirit, that for such a long time

had not been in her presence, trembling,
awestruck, still without the knowledge of sight,
touched just by the hidden virtue moving from her,
felt once again the power of my old love.
As soon as that high virtue struck my sight,
a power that had transfixed me from the time
I exited from boyhood, suddenly I wheeled
toward my left side, feeling that concern
a child has who rushes to his mamma
when he's afraid or when he is afflicted,
saying to Vergil: "Less than a single drop
of blood is left inside that isn't trembling;
I recognize the marks of that old flame."
But Vergil—he had left us—gone—
Vergil, sweetest father! Vergil to whom
I offered up myself for my salvation.
And all the tears our Ancient Mother shed
did not help my cheeks, freshly bathed by dew,
from being stained again by newer tears.
"Dante! just because your Vergil's gone,
don't be crying now; and yet you'll cry—
you'll cry as you feel the switch of another blade."

The words are those of a cold schoolmistress. They reflect some of
the allegorical frigidity of the Lady Philosophy of Boethius, upon
whom some of the characterization of Beatrice is modeled.[5] Beatrice
continues to make her accusations in lines 115 onward:

"This man had such potential in his youth (*vita nova*)
that every rightly taken habit of his
would have come to a miraculous proof.
But the wilder and the more malignant
is the soil sown with evil seed or left untilled,
whenever it has good earthy vigor in it.
For a time I sustained him with my look;
casting my youthful eyes upon him
I led him with me down the right-taken road.
But as soon as I stood upon the threshold
of the second phase of life, and changed my life,
this one tore away from me, giving himself to another.
And when I rose out of flesh to spirit,
and beauty and virtue kept increasing in me,
to him I became less dear, less welcome.
And he turned his paces down a way not true,
seeking after images of falseness
which never render promises entire.

It didn't help me then to offer inspirations
with which I wanted to recall him in sleep
or any other way; so little did he heed me!
So low he fell that every argument
was vain that could lead him toward his health,
except to show him the losses of the damned."

The woman to whom Beatrice is referring here is undoubtedly that
"lady young and very beautiful" who appeared at a window in *Vita
Nuova* XXXV to comfort Dante, and who, in effect, replaced Beatrice for a time in the poet's heart. If we go to the *Convivio*, we learn
that Dante read Cicero and Boethius after Beatrice's death. We can
thus see the way in which the temptress-Philosophy syndrome is
formed.[6]

   This correlation is intensified in *Purgatorio* XXXI.44 f. when
Beatrice mentions Dante's *errore* (either sin or wandering) and likens
it to the calls of Sirens. She also speaks of a "little chit of a girl"
(pargoletta) in line 59 and some other "novelty" *(novità)* in line 60
(some texts have *vanità,* "vanity"). Dante suggests, therefore, a
double sin: he forgot the ideal Beatrice for a series of women (we
should recall Boccaccio's statement that lust was the poet's greatest
problem); and further, in searching for direction in life, he immersed
himself in secular knowledge, neglecting the grand theological design. Only when he again found the design did he rediscover his
poetry. For the real, living Beatrice who resents other chits of girls is
also that *figura* for a concerned universe in which the highest souls of
the saved are in constant touch with those who are wandering.[7] The
mere jealousy of troubadour ethic is transferred into the much higher
notion of a lady's Christian caring. Just as a vitalized theology drives
away an arid philosophy, so the crowning image of this beautiful
woman (whom Pound calls a Reina or Aphrodite) expels the many
single manifestations of which she, as Beauty, is the perfection.

   Reason is extremely limited. Dante lets us know this through the
pathetic figure of Vergil slipping off into the shadows. The pragmatist,
the realistic thinker, is never going to advance to the symbolic
pageant in the Earthly Paradise, for he would find that ritual either
incomprehensible or absurd. The man who is wedded to reason alone
can never enter the true realms of heavenly light. This is a difficult act
that Pound himself had to face both in his writing and in his life. While
posing as Uncle Ez, he could lecture on politics and economics, and

in general employ a rock-drilling device, but when it came to visions of celestial order, that was another matter.[8] The question of both Pound's and Dante's ability to envision an end while not losing touch with the means to achieve it hinges to a large part upon their treatment of Guido Cavalcanti, who will be discussed more fully in the next two chapters.

For now, we can close the summary of Dante's development by saying that if Beatrice and what she represents (Theology) together illuminated the end of the design that was to serve as the basic architectonic for Dante's masterwork, it is Vergil who unquestionably gave Dante the visualized, imagistic approach from the human level. How did Dante dream up the form of the *Comedy?* Probably rather simply. For as Scartazzini said a long time ago: "The form of a journey through the realms of the next world was suggested to him by the age in which he lived; the literature of that age is so full of visions of the future state, of descriptions in prose and poetry of the torments and the bliss of eternity, that it were childish to ask which of these visions and legends Dante may have known and used."[9]

Simply using the consequences of the assumptions made above, we can see that he had Beatrice as his goal; she represents Heaven. Using the other two parts of the Christian Neoplatonic scheme, he needed to imagine the realms of Matter (Senses, Dianoia, Hyle) as Hell and Reason or Logos as Purgatory—what Pound referred to very loosely as the "Aquinas map." Since we have been discussing Dante from the point of view of Erigena, a staunch Neoplatonist, we can already dispense with a great deal of the cliché of Dante as a mere servant to St. Thomas. As every student of medieval philosophy knows, Thomism built upon Augustinianism and Neoplatonism in precisely the way that Aristotle assumed much of Plato.[10]

To approach the problem through our other major figure, Vergil, we could even say that the *Aeneid* showed the way to the *Comedy* as clearly as any medieval source did.[11] For in Book VI, Dante could see the hellish city of Dis that could be expanded into his Inferno at large; he could see fields of praise, which he could adapt to his Terrestrial Paradise and then, by Neoplatonic abstraction, into his Celestial Paradise. In between these two poles of salvation and damnation, a kind of humdrum workaday world that might have revealed itself more outside of the Underworld in the construction of the city of Rome may have suggested Purgatory, which is, after all, a continuation of life, a purification of its stains. Life to Vergil, as Dante probably interpreted it, was a hard, rugged road toward the forging of a holy city, the symbol of a Paradise on Earth. The Roman's "vale of tears" and the Florentine's wandering road of exile both led in some respect to Rome, as indeed Pound thought his direction lay in the 1930's. Without pressing further, we can see that in asking a basic question, we have found the answers that Dante himself gives us: in answer to his quest for aim, the two voices which spoke to him were the woman he most loved and the author he most revered.

Pound's problems as a designer of epic order were, of course, much more difficult. He wrote to R. P. Blackmur in 1924 that "one can no longer put Mt. Purgatory forty miles high in the midst of Australian sheep land" (*Letters*, p. 190), and he said in a letter to John Lackay Brown in 1937, "Stage set à la Dante is *not* modern truth. It may be O. K. but *not* as modern man's" (p. 293). He completed his dismissal of the Dantesque cosmology and its supposed Thomistic background in a letter written in 1939 to Hubert Creekmore: "I haven't an Aquinas-map; Aquinas *not* valid now" (*Letters*, p. 323). Since the form of the *Comedy* was impossible to duplicate in the modern world, and since the novel or any other narrative-oriented base seemed to be as unsuited to Pound as the writing of an Arthurian romance was to Dante, where could the form come from? This was a problem from the start, and it is even a problem for many of Pound's sympathetic critics today. Pound's detractors claim, of course, that he never found an adequate solution.[12]

To go to Pound's own words, he said in 1962: "I began the *Cantos* about 1904, I suppose. I had various schemes, starting in 1904 or 1905. The problem was to get a form—something elastic enough to take the necessary material . . . . Obviously you haven't got a nice little road map such as the middle ages possessed of Heaven. Only a musical form would take the material, and the Confucian universe as I see it is a universe of interacting strains and tensions."[13] A musical order and a Confucian cosmology involving the interaction of light and dark were thus the kinds of arrangement that Pound had in mind—at least at the end of the process. Yet the fact that Dante was not forgotten bulks large in remarks made shortly after the above: "You had six centuries that hadn't been packaged. It was a question of dealing with material that wasn't in the *Divina Commedia.*"

Dante had used a journey to bind together his judgements, and Pound, without a road map, had to find a way of finding a way. Yet let us not believe for a moment that Pound felt himself totally cut off from the Florentine. He said in *The Spirit of Romance* (p. 128): "There is little doubt that Dante conceived the real Hell, Purgatory, and Paradise as states, and not places. Richard St. Victor had, somewhile before, voiced this belief, and it is, moreover, a part of the esoteric and mystic dogma." Actually, it was Scotus Erigena who made the most out of dismissing the locality of states of soul after death—to the point of being declared a heretic many years later.[14] The point is: Dante did not, according to Pound, insist on foisting his own vision upon the world as anything *but* a vision, and he was therefore in the same position as Pound, except that his age had rather clear-cut notions of ethical judgement, and the literal-minded were willing to extend these frontiers to fixed places after death, thereby supplying points for a narrative line. Pound's dilemma was that he lived with men who no longer either had this ignorance or this faith—depending on one's point of view.

Therefore, as he said in the remarks above, Pound's impulse all along was to use a musical organization, for music implies design but not fixed locality. It has order, but the order is not susceptible to graphing, even if it does yield to notation. One must "play it by ear." Pound saw a kinsmanship here too with Dante, for he said in *The Spirit of Romance* (p. 177): "Dante lives in his mind; to him two blending thoughts give a music perceptible as two blending notes of a lute. He is in the real sense an idealist. He sings of true pleasures; he sings as exactly as Villon; they are admirably in agreement." In the same book, he said that Dante "sought to hang his song from the absolute, the center and source of light; art since Dante has for the most part built from the ground" (p. 166). He was keenly aware, then, that he was in the same fix as Villon; he was a post-medieval man, yearning for the absolute, yet stranded on the ground. Any journey that he took would have to proceed in terms of the earth's formation.

We might now make a jump and speak of how Pound tried to attack the immediate problem of the thread to hold his episodes together. In 1917, the summer of which saw the publication of the first three now-discarded Cantos appear in *Poetry,* Pound wrote to the lawyer and patron of artists John Quinn that he had begun work on a "new long poem (really LONG, endless, leviathanic)": *(Letters,* p.

104). His letter to Harriet Monroe accompanying the cantos shows his own sense of doubt: "Let us hope you may get over your dislike of the poem by the time the last of it is printed" (p. 110). Miss Monroe was not the only person who disliked the beginning of the new epic. In fact, after a few more cantos were published, Pound himself came to detest the abortive start as being too prolix, centerless, and falsely imitative of Browning's *Sordello*. The first three cantos, as they were printed in 1917, open with the famous interjection: "Hang it all, there can be but the one 'Sordello' '' and go on to express the dilemma of the author:[15]

> . . . and say the thing's an art-form,
> Your "Sordello"; and that the "modern world"
> Needs such a rag-bag to stuff its thought in;
> Say that I dump my catch, shiny and silvery
> As fresh sardines flapping and slipping on the marginal cobbles?

Whatever the modern world needed, it was not a rag-bag or a mess of sardines (shades of Dante's "hairy" words!). No, the problem of general form could not be so easily avoided.

We do not know exactly when the idea of a voyage of the mind became the answer to the problem, but that is what happened. Pound pulled his translation of Book XI of Homer's *Odyssey* from the Latin of Andreas Divus out of old Canto 3 and moved it into new Canto 1. In other words, Pound faced the problem of form squarely, instead of trying to take the easier road of writing satire or espousing artistic nihilism.[16] Homer offered an answer to the puzzle offered by Dante. Pound would proceed on his visionary journey the way a Greek or Phoenician sailor did, using the principle of sailing by ' περιπλους (*periplum* in Pound's Latin transferral): that is, by a direct confrontation with the earth gained by coasting around on it, rather than by using a celestial map to impose over it.[17] The stars were out there, but one had a coast at hand. Pound could accept the presence of gods, but he believed that one had to concentrate on what one could study.

This methodology was entirely in keeping with that of three of the lodestars that Pound later established as his "Sextant" in *Kulchur* (p. 352). Three figures who had worked primarily within the world or at least without the assumptions of a divine Überblick coloring their world-views were:

> 1. Confucius. Pound saw Confucianism moving from a concept of man as a social animal outwardly, from the *Analects* to the *Rites*. He was thus unlike Thomas Aquinas, who posited God and then sought to prove him.[18]

2. Louis Agassiz. This scientist who had taught at Harvard was, along with Von Humboldt, Leibnitz, and other men who were dedicated to empirical truth, a propounder of the idea that one must know in order to believe. In keeping with Scotus Erigena's words so often quoted by Pound, they all believed that "Authority comes from right reason; not the other way around."[19]
3. Leo Frobenius. The German anthropologist studied societies from within, without preconceived value judgements; he uncovered their *paideumas* or root ideas, and studied them as organisms which wax and wane, with "culture" as their fruit.[20]

    Thus the problem of artistic form was solved. If we think of the individual cantos as points on a chart in a voyage of the mind, we are not far from wrong. We can also conceive of them as various seats in the arena of history, from which we derive varying prospects.[21] We might further envision them as the laboratory slides that Agassiz would display, or even as movie strips, for we know from Mary de Rachewiltz' memoirs how much her father loved the cinema, and we have Walt Disney, the Disney both of nature films and childhood fantasy, enthroned in the later cantos.[22] With no Mount Purgatory to stand on and no lecture from Beatrice from the Moon, we must proceed from what we know. The *Cantos* are in one sense a do-it-yourself epic, with certain guidelines provided, but also with the opportunity provided to read the compass differently from the way the author does. After all, is the Mitteleuropa of Canto 35 really so bad? There is a Mitteleuropa ideogram consisting of Bach, Mozart, Innsbruck, and Walther von der Vogelweide, as well as that of Freud, Strauss, Vienna, and the Habsburgs. Not the slightest advantage of the *Cantos* is that it allows the reader to think. As Pound himself said: "Dante wrote his poems to MAKE PEOPLE THINK" *(Essays,* p. 204). For although we are accustomed nowadays to accept Dante's judgements as something short of gospel, was he really just with Philip the Fair? One doubts that Popes Boniface VIII or Nicholas III would vouch for his sense of justice. And similarly, what about the famous Aquinas map? Was Purgatory charted down to the last rung? Did every man in Italy know that there were nine circles in Hell, and who was in the eighth one? Let us not be foolish. Dante is far more imaginative and daring than his pious, all-accepting modern commentators would have us believe.

    In the period from 1917 to the publication of *A Draft of XVI Cantos* by the Three Mountains Press in Paris eight years later, Pound reworked the first eight cantos constantly. Having decided upon a loose, malleable form of organization, he was still faced with the problem of moral order. Dante was making judgements in his poem in three degrees. Was Pound to settle simply for varying shades of light and dark, as he had suggested with respect to Confucius, or should he try to formalize his distinctions? His anxiety is expressed in a letter to his old professor friend, Felix Schelling, in 1922: "Having the crust to attempt a poem in 100 or 120 cantos long after all mankind has been commanded never again to attempt a poem of any length, I have to stagger as I can" *(Letters,* p. 180). Then, almost as if anticipating the various outcries of incoherence against the cantos published to that date, he added: "The first 11 cantos are preparation of the palette. I *have* to get down all the colours or elements I want for the poem. Some perhaps too enigmatically and abbreviatedly. I hope, heaven help me, to bring them into some sort of design and architecture later." It is interesting to note that here he was thinking of his work in terms of art, or as he said in the abortive Canto I, he wanted to "write to paint, not music,/ O Casella" *(Lustra,* p. 187).

The analogy of music or art was never clear in his own mind in the 1920's, for he said in a letter to Homer Pound in 1927 that the structure of the new work was "Rather like, or unlike subject and response and counter subject in fugue" *(Letters,* p. 210). This idea was echoed by William Butler Yeats in *A Packet for Ezra Pound* when he said, with 27 cantos then completed, that the over-all work would "display a structure like that of a Bach Fugue."[23] Pound howled out later against this remark *(Letters,* p. 321), but he seemed to be objecting more to Yeats' obfuscating style than to the truth of the statement. For Yeats made matters more complicated by switching to art for an analogy in a passage that deserves to be quoted at length:[24]

He has scribbled on the back of an envelope certain sets of letters that represent emotions or archetypal events—I cannot find any adequate definition—ABCD and then JKLM, and then each set of letters repeated, and then ABCD inverted and this repeated, and then a new element XYZ, then certain letters that never recur, and then all sorts of combinations of XYZ and JKLM and ABCD and DCBA, and all set whirling together. He has shown me upon the wall a photograph of a Cosimo Tura decoration in three compartments, in the upper the Triumph of Love and the Triumph of Chastity, in the middle Zodiacal signs, and in the lower certain events in Cosimo Tura's day. The Descent and the Metamorphosis—ABCD and JKLM—his fixed elements, took the place of the Zodiac, the archetypal persons—XYZ—that of the Triumphs, and certain modern events—his letters that do not recur—that of those events in Cosimo Tura's day.

Out of this rather garbled prose comes a strange sense of order. Yeats is referring to the Room of the Months in the Schifanoia Palace created for the Este family in Ferrara by the painters Francesco del Cossa and Cosimo Tura. The subjects there fall into three levels, as Guy Davenport has shown, with the lowest one showing real people working their ways upward through various cycles to the creation of a social order.[25] This general division is fully applicable to Pound's *Cantos*, for the poet himself declared: "I was not following the three divisions of the *Divine Comedy* exactly. One can't follow the Dantesquan cosmos in an age of experiment. But I have made the division between people dominated by emotion, people struggling upwards, and those who have some part of the divine vision. The thrones in Dante's *Paradiso* are for the spirits of the people who have been responsible for good government. The thrones in the *Cantos* are an attempt to move out from egoism and to establish some definition of an order possible or at any rate conceivable on earth."[26] This remark not only supports what Yeats said about the Del Cossa-Tura paintings, but it also aligns Pound's form of judgement with Dante's, and it accords with Pound's own ideas about medieval thinking, which he derived in *Kulchur* (p. 77) from Richard of St. Victor's epistemology.[27] Richard, according to Pound, pictured thought as moving on three ascending levels: 1) cogitation: the mind flitting aimlessly about an object; 2) meditation: the mind methodically circling something that endures; and 3) contemplation: the mind and the object one, when "we become the thing we know."

Both the Schifanoia murals and the Victorine epistemology suggest three gradations of being: 1) something shifting, passing; 2) something recurrent; and 3) something perpetual. We can now bring back into play the tripartite Neoplatonic structure developed by Scotus Erigena, noting how closely the units accord with what we have already established. In the Erigenistic framework we have: 1) Nous or Spirit, perpetual and enduring at the top; 2) Logos or Reason working as an intermediary, sometimes hindered in its performance, but nevertheless present as a link with the divine; and finally 3) Dianoia or Hyle, Matter, what Pound calls in the foregoing passage "emotions" and "egoism," that which is here for a time but does not endure. Thus we have constructed an ideogram from medieval epistemology, Renaissance art, and Neoplatonic metaphysics. We have, in fact, the three divisions for what could be the three canticles of The Great Modern Epic.

These musical movements or artistic panels were clarified in 1932 when Pound wrote to John Drummond: "Best div. prob. the permanent, the recurrent, the casual" *(Letters*, p. 239). The three divisions are traceable back to a series of articles published in the *New Age* in 1912 and much later issued as the book *Patria Mia.*[28] As Pound's recent explicator Clark Emery has pointed out, these are probably the safest guidelines to use for the general form of the *Cantos.*[29]

It is important to establish these three divisions at this time, for we shall refer to them throughout the course of this study. It is also important to affirm Pound's own words recorded above that he has not employed a strict tripartite canticle division within the work. This is the mistake committed by Daniel D. Pearlman in his recent study, where he divides his own work into units which are supposed to follow Pound's Hell (Cantos 1 to 30), his Purgatory (31 to 71), and his Paradise (74-84), with the later cantos acting as fields for reprises.[30] Pearlman is perfectly well aware of the dangers involved, but he frequently falls back into this overly simplified pattern. Indeed it is a difficult one to avoid. In this study for purposes of clarity, I shall use the following neutral names: Early Cantos for 1 to 30, Middle Cantos for 31 to 71, and Later Cantos for the rest.

One can see that any attempt to reconcile Pound neatly with Dante is wrong by looking at the broad design. In the middle of the first thirty cantos, we do, in fact, have a two-canto sequence which Pound himself in his 1927 letter to his father called his infernal section: "You have had a hell in Canti XIV, XV; purgatorio in XVI etc." *(Letters*, p. 210). Similarly in a letter to Wyndham Lewis, he speaks of "the two cantos dealing with Hell" *(Letters*, p. 191), but it is significant that only two are cited in this respect. Everyone agrees that the famous Confucius Canto, 13, is a prelude to Pound's Heaven, and Pound himself spoke of Canto 20 as containing a "general paradiso" *(Letters*, p. 210). Similarly, in the *Pisan Cantos* states of mind shift abruptly from the pain of reality to the comfort of ideal forms:

Le Paradis n'est pas artificiel
but spezzato apparently
it exists only in fragments unexpected excellent sausage,
the smell of mint, for example,
Ladro the night cat;

(Canto 74/438:465)

Of course it is tempting to try to impose Dante's structure on Pound, and perhaps there is rightness in saying that there is *more* of a Hell in the first 30 cantos than in the rest of the poem, and so on. In fact, Pound in his later years took to speaking of his *Rock-Drill* and *Thrones* as his *Paradiso*.[31] But for the most part, we must resist any clear-cut divisions.

At least one other facet of the work must be considered at this point: the musical movements that Pound himself suggested to his father in 1927 (*Letters*, p. 210):

> A.   A.   Live man goes down into world of Dead
> C.   B.   The "repeat in history"
> B.   C.   The "magic moment" or moment of metamorphosis,
>   bust thru from quotidien into "divine or
>   permanent world." Gods, etc.

This scheme, which was also suggested by Yeats' prose, has caused perhaps more discussion than it is worth, for there is little in this fugal pattern that is not implied in the divisions which have emerged above. The magic moment is, of course, the indication of Paradise. The "repeat" is the recurrent element that we have associated with a Purgatory. The descent in A is more than the visit to the Underworld with which the poem opens (indeed, in one sense most of the *Cantos* take place in a shadowland of the past).

As one proceeds in the *Cantos*, it is obvious that other patterns emerge. For example, we may see the entire voyage as one leading to the formation of an ideal city, which Pound calls at times the city of King Dioce (Deiokes), Ecbatan(a), from Herodotus (I.98), or the city of Wagadu, which is taken from the legend of the African Soninke tribe; Wagadu is a city that will fall and be rebuilt four times.[32] The ideal composite will be a city with four walls, for Pound finds in the number four, especially in Chinese characters, the nature of solidity, something that will stand:

>   Faasa !   4 times was the city remade,
>   now in the heart indestructible
>   4 gates, the 4 towers

                                                    (Canto 77/465:494)

or again:

    But the four TUAN
                    are from nature
        jen, i, li, chih
    Not from descriptions in the school house;
    They are the scholar's job,
                    the gentleman's and the officer's.

                                                    (Canto 99/711:740)

Over the Earthly Paradise is the number three, exerting a magic charm as it does in Dante's terza rima, his three canticles, and the constant repetitions of Trinities and triads in his work. To Pound the three itself takes on many forms of linkage, as in these groupings of honored people:

Mozart, Agassiz and Linnaeus	(Canto 113)
Webster, Voltaire and Leibnitz	(Canto 104)
Mencius, Dante, and Agassiz	(Canto 94)

The triads are not restricted to doers and thinkers like those cited above, but can work in a way that embraces the infernal as well as the paradisal, just as they do in Dante:

    The hells move in cycles,
                    No man can see his own end.
    The Gods have not returned. "They have never left us."
                    They have not returned.
    Cloud's processional and the air moves with their living.
    Pride, jealousy and possessiveness
                    3 pains of hell
    and a clear wind over garofani
                    over Portofino 3 lights in triangulation
                                                    (Canto 113/787)

Thus Yeats was not at all wrong when he stressed the numerical importance of three and four in his *Packet*.[33]

    In conclusion, we must admit that Pound himself was often racked with doubt about the question of order in his poem. For a time he refused to use the word "epic" in describing it, preferring the neutral "long poem," *(Letters,* p. 189). In *The Spirit of Romance* he had said that the *Divine Comedy* itself was not an epic, but a collection of lyrics (p. 153); and in the same place he decided that the *Commedia* was really a cycle of mystery plays, as was quoted earlier. In one sense, this observation on Dante's dramatic composition is brilliant; but in another sense it is a dodge, for the *Comedy,* as Francis Fergusson has shown, has a genuine Aristotelian rhythm: a graspable protagonist, a coherent narrative line, and a visible beginning, middle, and end.[34]

In his youthful *Spirit of Romance* (p. 216), long before any problem of epic structure had appeared to trouble his mind, Pound uttered some words about the Portuguese writer Camoens which might well haunt the rest of this study: "An epic cannot be written against the grain of its time: the prophet or the satirist may hold himself aloof from his time, or run counter to it, but the writer of epos must voice the general heart." For a while, Pound seems to have been teased by the notion that perhaps the novel was the form best adapted for doing this.[35] But after his studies of James, Flaubert, and others, he came increasingly to the conclusion that only poetry was capable of expressing the most highly idealized dreams of man. He believed that he had positive things to say, in a way that Wyndham Lewis, Yeats, and even Eliot did not: "But the lot of 'em, Yeats, Possum, Old Wyndham/ had no ground to stand on" (Canto 102/728:754).

In pursuing Pound's search for his epic-to-be, the reader may have become aware that the empirical methodology that Pound settled for clashes to some extent with the Neoplatonic framework that is often employed as a cosmological scheme for the *Cantos.* How, for example, can Pound employ the techniques of Aristotle, Agassiz, and Leibnitz while at the same time holding on to the visions of Erigena, Plotinus, and Psellos? In other words, the *Cantos* run directly into the age-old dichotomy of realism and idealism, presenting us with a problem that must be faced. But the reconciliation of reality with an idealistic vision was a problem for Dante too. And, curiously enough, it is in the figure of Guido Cavalcanti—Dante's best friend and one of Pound's favorite translation figures—that this problem can be best studied and resolved.

4

CAVALCANTI AS MENTOR

It is hard to say which of our poets was more greatly influenced by Guido Cavalcanti. In Chapter III of the *Vita Nuova* Dante tells us that his literary career was launched when Guido replied to one of his early sonnets about Beatrice. Here at the very start of the work Dante pays Guido the tribute of calling him "the first of my friends." In Chapter XXV, where Dante goes through an elaborate explanation of metaphor, which he calls "the poet's allegory," he again aligns himself with his first friend against dolts—presumably Bonagiunta, Guittone, and others who do not understand the precepts of "the sweet new style." In Chapter XXX, Cavalcanti is mentioned as the major instigator for Dante's writing in Italian rather than in Latin. Although this citation is often brushed by, it shows that Guido was firmly opposed to the traditional rhetoric of the Establishment, an opposition that forebode ill. Another mention occurs in Chapter XXIV of the *Vita Nuova*, where Dante describes Beatrice walking in the streets of Florence behind Cavalcanti's girl, who is called Primavera (which means either Spring or "she will come first"), whose real name was Giovanna. Dante overlays the event with allegorical significance, likening Giovanna (the feminine form of Giovanni or John) to John the Baptist, who preceded Christ; Beatrice, of course, soars in stature through the analogy.

Even if we did not have these personal attestations, we could assume a strong bond between the two contemporaries. Dante salutes Guido along with their mutual friend Lapo Gianni in the so-called

"Invitation to a Magic Ride." This is one of the finest lyrics that Dante ever wrote, but is not very well-known because it was not contained in the *Vita Nuova,* probably because the woman in line 10 who "looms above the thirty best" does not seem to be Beatrice:[1]

> Guido, I wish that you and Lapo and I,
> Spirited on the wings of a magic spell,
> Could drift in a ship where every rising swell
> Would sweep us at our will across the skies.
> Then tempest never, nor any weather dire
> Could ever make our blissful living cease;
> No, but abiding in a steady, blessèd peace
> Together we'd share the increase of desire.
> And Lady Vanna and Lady Lagia then
> And she who looms above the thirty best
> Would join us at the good enchanter's behest;
> And there we'd talk of Love without an end
> To make those ladies happy in the sky—
> With Lapo enchanted too, and you and I.

Here we catch the feeling of the brilliant world of medieval romanticism before Dante and his circle brought it so close to the structure of the Church. We have Merlin, magic sorcerers, and flying ships, as fantasy is loosed in a quasi-metaphysical cosmos. If Dante was to later suppress this kind of writing, it is as much a loss for poetry as it was a gain for his intellectual maturity.

Guido also wrote a number of poems in which he mentions his friend. Sonnet XXIV in Pound's *Translations* is addressed "Dante, I pray thee, if thou Love discover" (p. 73). In it, Guido begs Alighieri to tell him if their mutual friend Lapo Gianni is truly a servant of Love, or if he is a mere pretender. The sonnet assumes a whole social ambience for the mystique of love: was this circle merely literary, or did it also have political and economic interests? This question haunted Pound.[2] Aside from the previously mentioned Sonnet XXII, which Guido proffered vainly as an answer to Dante's first oracular poem of the *Vita Nuova,* we have Sonnet XXIX, which in Pound's translation reveals much of the tortured, tragic language of love that one finds in the opening chapters of the *Vita Nuova:*

> Dante, a sigh, that's the heart's messenger
> Assailed me suddenly as I lay sleeping,
> Aroused, I fell straightway into fear's keeping,
> For Love came with that sigh as curator.

The rhetoric here clearly indicates the role that Cavalcanti played in shaping Dante's youthful poetry.
What of the life of this best friend of Alighieri? Pound himself gathered the meager facts in the preface of his 1912 edition of *The Sonnets and Ballate of Guido Cavalcanti,* which was reprinted in his *Translations* as follows:[3]

> Born 1250 (circa), his mother probably of the Conti Guidi. In 1266 or 1267 'Cavalcante dei Cavalcanti gave for wife to his son Guido one of the Uberti, ' i.e., the daughter of Farinata. Thus Villani. . . . We may set 1283 as the date of his reply to Dante's first sonnet. In 1284 he was a member of the grand council with Dino Compagni and Brunetto Latino. In party feuds of Florence Guelf, then a 'White' with the Cherci [Cerchi], and most violent against Corso Donati. 1292-96 is the latitude given us for the pilgrimage to the holy house of Galicia. Corso, it is said, tried to assassinate him on this pilgrimage. . . . upon his return from the pilgrimage which had extended only to Toulouse, Guido attacks Corso in the streets of Florence, and for the general turmoil ensuing, the leaders of both factions were exiled.

We have already mentioned Guido's exile to Sarzana, his tardy recall, and his death by fever back in his native city, which Villani dates August 29, 1300. In his *Cronica* VIII.42, Villani called Guido "a philosopher, and skilled in many things, although somewhat oversensitive *(tenero)* and fiery *(stizzoso)*." Dino Compagni, who knew Guido well, called him in his history (I.20) a "noble *cavaliere* . . . well-mannered and bold, but arrogant and given to aloneness and bent on his studies."

The classical portrait of Guido occurs in Boccaccio's *Decameron* as the Ninth Tale of the Sixth Day, where he is described as being "one of the best logicians in the world" and "a very fine natural philosopher," a man who was most witty, charming, and facile of tongue. The tale is merely a brief anecdote in which some bores led by Betto Brunelleschi attempted to waylay Guido, who was walking alone, musing among some tombs around the Church of San Giovanni in Florence. When the men tried to detain Guido by the teasing words, "When you find that God doesn't exist, what will you have done?" he leapt over a marble tomb and shouted back: "Milords, you can say anything you want about me inside your own houses." At first the men were puzzled, but finally they realized that "their own houses" must be the graves where they were standing at that moment, and that Guido was quite literally consigning them to the Hell of the non-intellectual, where they already were. Elissa, who tells the tale, makes the Gothic background of death and disintegration all the more dramatic by her prefatory comment that Guido "believed in some of the ideas of the *epicurii*" (Epicureans, but also in a broader sense, heretics), and that therefore the masses thought that the prime purpose of his speculations was "to prove that God does not exist." Pound heartily approved of this separation of Guido from the main Christian tradition. He noted that Guido's work was part of "the radiant world where one thought cuts through another with clean edge, a world of moving energies," and a world that was "untouched by the two maladies, the Hebrew disease, the Hindoo disease, fanaticisms and excess that produce Savonarola, asceticisms that produce fakirs, St Clement of Alexandria, with his prohibition of bathing by women" *(Essays,* p. 154).

The association of the Cavalcantis with free, easy living is borne out by Dante's treatment of them in the *Comedy.* Naturally Guido does not appear as a shade, since the vision of the poem occurs in the spring of 1300 and he was still alive. But the father of the house, Cavalcante, is a major character in *Inferno* X, along with the lordly Farinata degli Uberti, the father of Guido's wife, Bice or Beatrice.[4] This is the Circle of Heretics, where the damned are suffering in massively impressive, detached sepulchers. Epicurus himself is mentioned as a resident of the place, both for his atheism and undoubtedly for his hedonistic doctrines.[5]

We enter the scene with a very long prelude in which the hellish fires of the City of Dis are described with dramatic energy. To complete the scene, we have allegorical Furies perching on the walls of the town, and finally a guardian angel who must be summoned to help Vergil clear the way. The medieval drama that unfolds stresses the ineffectuality of Reason to cope with Heresy by itself, for Reason is the victim of this intellectual sin. Once the way has been cleared, Dante moves along speaking to Vergil, when suddenly he is interrupted by the voice of the once mighty Farinata, who speaks with him rather arrogantly until:

> There arose then a shade, along beside him,
> hidden from my sight beneath the chin
> (indeed, I think he was raised up on his knees).
> He stared around me, as if he had the desire
> to see if there was someone who was with me;

and when his expectations were exhausted,
crying, he said: "If you go passing through
this blind prison because of your high genius,
my son—where's he? Why isn't he here with you?"
And I to him: "I didn't come here by myself.
That man over there who's waiting leads me—
that man your Guido held perhaps in disdain."
His words and the very nature of his pain
had already made apparent to me his name;
and so my reply was full of cogent facts.
Suddenly he reared up, crying: "'Held'?
What—you said 'held'? Isn't he living now?
Isn't the blessèd light still striking his eyes?"
And when he realized that there was some delay
that I was making in confrontation with his plea,
supine he fell, and never came up again.

Most of the best commentators on this passage like Auerbach are keen in pointing out the dramatic way in which the one voice slices through the other.[6] The two imprisoned men are completely different. Farinata was a Ghibelline, and Cavalcante was a Guelf. Farinata was primarily a man of military deeds, and Cavalcante inclined to philosophical speculation and the fine art of living. The way in which Cavalcante is portrayed in humble, pathetic terms, as opposed to the lordly Farinata, may express the sympathy that Dante held for the Cavalcanti clan. After all, heresy is a very special sin, not one of the Seven Deadly. The heretics are far more aristocratic and refined than are the wrathful who precede them or the tyrants who follow them. It is clear from the dramatic way in which the canto is constructed, especially with the elaborate prelude, that Dante was much concerned with this "sin" and this group of people. It is also clear from the way that the son is brought into the discussion that Guido may well be running the risk of ending in the same woeful estate as his father.

A rift between Cavalcanti and Dante has been documented in a sharp poem of rebuke by Guido, numbered as Sonnet XXIII in Pound's *Translations:*

I daily come to thee uncounting times
And find thee ever thinking over vilely;
Much doth it grieve me that thy noble mind
And virtue's plenitude are stripped from thee.

Io vengo il giorno a te infinite volte,
E trovoti pensar troppo vilmente;
Molto mi duol de la gentil tua mente,
E d'assai tue virtù, che ti son tolte.

Was this sonnet written after Beatrice's death, as Pound believed, or was it written, perhaps more plausibly, as Leonardo Vitetti has suggested, when Guido saw his friend Dante falling into the loose style of living *(vilmente)* that Beatrice suggested in her diatribe on Mount Purgatory?[7] Was Dante himself an Epicurean, at least in the hedonistic sense? How ironic it is to entertain the possibility that Dante fell into the easy, luxurious life of Florence and then pulled himself out, only to go on to accuse his closest friend of the same sin!

But I doubt that Guido's accusation refers merely to fat partridges and rich puddings, the kind of sybaritic life that Folgore of San Gimignano celebrated so exquisitely in his cycle of sonnets for the seasons.[8] No. Guido's care goes much deeper than that; and frankly, we shall probably never know exactly what caused it. The relationship between the two men was extremely intricate, consisting at times of warm, intimate friendship, and at other times of feelings of rivalry, and even jealousy and resentment. In our own day, we have the Pound-Eliot friendship as an analogue.

The letter that Pound sent Eliot with the return of the draft of *The Waste Land* in 1921 begins with the salutation "Caro mio" and contains a great deal of paternal talk, but it also says: "Complimenti, you bitch. I am wracked by the seven jealousies" *(Letters,* p. 169). When Eliot was called upon to review Pound's work, his praise of the *Cantos* was indeed mixed, consisting of such remarks as "I am glad that the philosophy is there, but I am not interested in it."[9] Eliot spoke of Pound as someone who had an "immense influence, but no disciples." He then launched on a full-scale attack upon Pound's ideology (how we wish that Dante had recorded what he felt about Guido!): "He retains some mediaeval mysticism, without belief; this is mixed up with Mr Yeats's spooks . . . and involved with Dr Berman's hormones; and a steam-roller of Confucian rationalism (the Religion of a Gentleman, and therefore an Inferior Religion) has flattened over the whole. So we are left with the question (which the unfinished Cantos make more pointed) what does Mr Pound believe?" The particulars cited are rather foolish, especially the attack on Confucius, but what affected Pound perhaps most of all was the tone. He brooded over the last question for many years, until he composed his pseudo-catechism, which he titled *Religio or, The Child's Guide to Knowledge*, which has been reprinted in *Pavannes and Divagations* (pp. 96 ff.). It begins as follows:

> What is a god?
> A god is an eternal state of mind.
> What is a faun?
> A faun is an elemental creature. . . .
> When is a god manifest?
> When the states of mind take form.
> When does a man become a god?
> When he enters one of these states of mind. . . .
> By what characteristic may we know the divine forms?
> By beauty.

Dante called Cavalcanti a heretic; Eliot called Pound a pagan, a seeker after exoticism, a denier of his Christian roots. Cavalcanti jibed at Dante for living *vilmente;* Pound ridiculed Eliot for being hypocritical (calling him Brother Possum, Reverend Eliot) and for being a hollow man.[10] If we had some of Cavalcanti's correspondence, especially had Guido lived to see some of the *Comedy* on parchment, would he not perhaps have teased his friend for being too orthodox in his philosophy, precisely the way that Pound jabbed at Dante for being *"diablement dans les idées reçues" (Essays*, p. 149)? One can only surmise.

The relationship between Dante and Guido was obviously every bit as intricate as that between Pound and Eliot. Dante saw his best friend die; indeed, he even took part in the decision to send him off into exile. Eliot saw his comrade incarcerated in a detention camp, indicted as a traitor, and then committed for years to an insane asylum while he was writing some of the most beautiful poetry in the English language. If the *De vulgari* was written late, as is assumed, then Dante clung to his notion of Guido as one of the world's greatest poets. His admiration of the *Donna mi prega* never left him, no matter what he thought of the philosophy behind it. Similarly, despite their political divergences, Eliot and Pound remained true to the principles which had originally brought them together. Ezra is reported to have muttered over the Possum's grave that, with him gone, "Who is there for me to share a joke with?"[11]

There is no doubt, however, that Dante decided at some point to put his friend's philosophy and style aside. The freethinking, free-wheeling poet-philosopher was simply treading on dangerous ground, and Dante at last concluded that he must not follow in his footsteps. I take the collapse of the *Convivio* as the expression of this falling out of infatuation with Philosophy per se, just as I would date the end of the most important effects of Guido's rhetoric upon the younger poet at the middle of the *Vita Nuova*, where Dante moved into the sphere of Guido Guinizelli and the Neoplatonic tenor of thought emanating from Bologna. When Dante opens the *Comedy,* he is a man who is prepared to substitute the action of grace symbolized by Beatrice's descent into Hell for any self-garnered illumination; Vergil, who represents among other things Reason, can act only when this divine *donum* has been extended.

At this point, it is perhaps important to answer that tiresome question about the *Comedy's* being "rhymed theology," if only because Pound himself has thrust the notion of Alighieri's servitude to Aquinas upon us. This idea was fashionable among Victorian critics like Paget Toynbee, whose influence on Pound we have already encountered in *Spirit.* Toynbee was capable of saying almost casually with reference to the *Summa Theologica* that "though he never quotes it by name, Dante was deeply indebted" to it, for its influence is "perceptible throughout his writings."[12]

Today we are skeptical about such an easy generalization. Etienne Gilson's brilliant and amusing book, *Dante the Philosopher,* ought to have dispelled once and for all the notion that Dante was anyone's slave. He did not shake off the effects of Cavalcanti merely to assume those of the man of Aquino, who was himself highly suspect in the thirteenth century. To back his argument, Gilson analyzed the philosophical points of the *Convivio,* the basic political outlook of the *De monarchia,* which we shall discuss in Chapter 6, and various points within the *Comedy* before asserting Dante's independence from one system; he even suggested a certain amount of originality. When Dante uses primary sources, he often makes them clear, as he showed in the case of Vergil. He does not in any place give any priority to St. Thomas. In fact, when he encounters the saint in Canto X of the *Paradiso,* Aquinas is balanced with St. Bonaventure in XII, an avowed Platonist in the opposing tradition of Augustine. Henry Osborn Taylor expressed the relationship among the three very succinctly when he said: "Dante is the child of the Middle Ages, rather than a disciple of any single teacher. If he follows Aquinas more than any other scholastic, he follows Bonaventura also with breadth and balance."[13] True, Taylor later qualifies this judgement when he says that when Dante thinks, "more frequently he thinks like Thomas." But did Thomas have a patent on the "intellectual realization of life" in his age? Only, perhaps, to us looking back with the comfort of retrospect.

Today, after the work of such scholars as Joseph Anthony Mazzeo and P. Pietro Chioccioni, who have clearly established Platonic foundations for the *Comedy,* we incline to a view of Dante's balance in his handling of tradition.[14] Dante took what he wanted when he wanted it, never shying from any source, no matter how sensitive. For example, Bruno Nardi has shown us that the account of the creation of the soul in Canto XXV of the *Purgatorio* leans toward the heretical.[15] Furthermore, Dante placed the heretic Sigier of Brabant in Paradise among the blessed with St. Thomas, just as he put the equally condemned Calabrese abbot Joachim of Fiore with Bonaventure in *Paradiso* XII. Let us not quash the poet's courage and imagination by chaining him to a man who may seem to us to have coined the age's thought, but who in his own perilous day was himself suspect. George Santayana, speaking on the quite defensible opposing side about Dante's Platonic nature, noted: "In some form or other Platonic ideas occur in all poetry of passion when it is seasoned with reflection."[16] Bravo. Then, with that literary sensitivity that is often rare with philosophers and historians, he added that the Platonism of Dante is "in any case, quite his own."

Dante never fully forgot Guido. In Canto XI of the *Purgatorio* the illuminator Oderisi of Gubbio pays Cavalcanti one of the finest tributes he ever received. Dante begins the passage with a salutation (79 ff.):

"O!" I said to him, "aren't you Oderisi,
the pride of Gubbio, the master of that art
they call illumination up in Paris?"
"Brother," said he, "now are laughing the pages
that were penned by Franco of Bologna.
The honor's all his; now just mine in part.
But never would I have been so courteous
while I was living, because of my great desire
for excellence, where all my heart was set.

But here I pay the fee for all that pride.
And I wouldn't even be here if it wasn't that,
in the midst of sin, I turned my face to God.
O vain glory of all the human prowess!
How little green shows itself on top,
and that's soon followed by an age that's gross.
They thought once Cimabue held the field
in painting, and now it's Giotto has the cry,
so that now the fame of the latter has grown dim.
The same way Guido the second from Guido first [Guinizelli]
snatched the glory of our tongue; and there'll be born
perhaps another who'll drive them both out of the nest."

Needless to say, the compliment to the second Guido (Cavalcanti)
has a decidedly two-edged cut. For we can well imagine who that
third person will be who will surpass his predecessors. But when Eliot
paid Pound the supreme compliment of dedicating *The Waste Land* to
him, was he not aware that the phrase *miglior fabbro* was bestowed
originally by a great and popular poet upon a man whom later genera-
tions have largely ignored?

5

CAVALCANTI AS MASK

Pound was interested in the poems of Guido Cavalcanti throughout his career. When we examine his direct uses of the Italian, we soon confront a problem that has both a philosophical and a poetic dimension. Frequently in the *Cantos* Pound aligns Guido through the Italian's light imagery with Neoplatonism, and his *amore* seems to acquire a transcendental feeling. To most critics, however, Guido is far closer to the opposing empirical tradition of Aristotelianism. Pound, we will find, also makes Guido serve this end. We must therefore ask ourselves in the course of this chapter if Pound the critic is fair in his assessment of the Italian, and we must bear in mind Pound the poet, with his freedom to make assertions through poetic inference that ignore the rules of discursive logic.

During his career Pound was engaged in at least six major presentations of Cavalcanti's work.[1] If we survey Pound's letters, we constantly find Guido's name coupled with that of Dante Alighieri.[2] In his *Spirit of Romance* Pound was careful to establish the greatness of the older poet, saying: "Dante himself never wrote more poignantly, or with greater intensity than Cavalcanti" (p. 110). In the same passage, however, this book shows a tendency to regard Guido as somewhat restricted: "A spirit more imperious and less subtle than Dante, more passionate, less likely to give ear to sophistries; his literary relation to Dante is not unlike Marlowe's to Shakespear, though such comparisons are always unsafe." When *Spirit* was re-edited in 1929, Pound changed this judgement a bit by adding the following note to the words "less subtle than Dante": "I retract this expression." Furthermore, in another interpolation in 1929, he increased Guido's claims by stating that "Dante is less in advance of his time than Guido Cavalcanti" (p. 132).

By the time that Pound was doing his concentrated study of Guido in the late twenties, he began to find Cavalcanti more and more attractive. Already in the Introduction to the 1912 edition of his poems, reprinted in *Translations,* he had said, "Than Guido Cavalcanti no psychologist of the emotions is more keen in his understanding, more precise in his expression" (p. 18). Two important criteria—precision in language and acuteness in observation—were thus observable in Cavalcanti's work. In fact, in his early work Pound saw Guido as an influence of some magnitude upon Dante. He said of the line "Then shalt thou see her virtue risen in heaven" from Ballata V of *Translations,* "I would go so far as to say that 'Il Paradiso' and the form of 'The Commedia' might date from this line; very much as I think I find in Guido's 'Place where I found people whereof each one grieved overly of Love,' some impulse that has ultimate fruition in Inferno V" (p. 19). Guido, then, was the lyricist who supplied some notion of general structure for Dante's epic.

When Pound's early editions of Cavalcanti were reissued in the deluxe edition of 1966, Pound worried about his own poetic renderings: "I am as aware as any of my critics that it is ridiculous to introduce a few obscure archaisms . . . and lopsided metaphors, as I did in the sonnets."[3] In the very first edition he did not translate the *Donna mi prega,* although that poem was added in 1931 and was subsequently reworked into the major portion of Canto 36. Also, he has never translated the beautiful *Fresca rosa novella* or some of the doubtfully attributed but interesting scientifically worded poems that occur in the Cicciaporci edition of 1813.[4] In examining Guido's work, we will put Pound's *Translations,* which follow his own edition of the Italian texts, next to the more recent editions of Giulio Cattaneo and Guido Favati.[5]

The first phase of Cavalcanti's work we might term the pastoral or, more properly, pastourelle period. This includes the lovely Sonnet XVII, which was written to Bernardo da Bologna allegedly to explain why the waters of Galicia are so sweet. The poem contains some memorable lines which Pound renders:

. . . I send Pinella a river in full flood

Stockèd with Lamia-nymphs, that are foreby
Served each with her slave hand-maids, fair to sight
And yet more fair by manner of gentlehood.

Mando io a la Pinella un grande fiume
Pieno di lamie, servito da schiave,
Belle, ed adorne di gentil costume.

This refrain occurs in a far more refined way in Canto 91/616:650:

'mand'io a la Pinella'
                    sd/ Guido
                                'a river',
'Ghosts dip in the crystal,
                    adorned'

It recurs in Canto 92/618:651, where a river full of pagan, Ovidian
forms is likened to the golden flow of Nous, as in Neoplatonic
philosophers such as Porphyry, Plotinus, Psellos, or Scotus Erigena,
and where the composite Egyptian god Ra-Set is pictured on a river:

Ra-Set in her barge now
                    over deep sapphire
but the child played under wave. . .
          e piove d'amor
          in nui
          a great river, the ghosts dipping in crystal
& to Pinella. . .

In another part of the modern epic the flow of the river is presented as a golden rain of love, which occurs in Ballata VII *(Trans.,*
pp. 110 ff.), rendered thus by Pound:

Being in thought of love I came upon
Two damsels strange
Who sang 'The rains
Of love are falling, falling within us.'

Era in pensier d'Amor, quand'io trovai
Due forosette nove:
L'una cantava: E' piove
Gioco d'Amore in nui.

The poem goes on to mention a beautiful girl named Mandetta from the city of Toulouse, who lived by the golden-roofed church of La Daurade. Cavalcanti apparently enjoyed her company while on a never-completed pilgrimage to Spain:

> *Speed Ballatet' unto Tolosa city*
> *And go in softly 'neath the golden roof.*

As we can see, the pagan nymphs who open this poem yield to a beautiful woman inside a sacred temple in a holy city (Toulouse to Pound was a much-admired Albigensian fortress). This ideogram of woman-temple-city is one of the major image clusters in the *Cantos*. Canto 4 speaks of the "church roof in Poictiers/ If it were gold" (14:18), thus bringing Duke William IX of Aquitaine, the first troubadour, into the picture. Canto 21/98:102 mentions that "Gold fades in the gloom,/ Under the blue-black roof, Placidia's," adding Ravenna to the complex. Guido's ladies and events from his life form a central part of this widening ideogram.

Perhaps the finest pastorella of Guido is the sensual Ballata IX (pp. 118 f.), *In un boschetto trovai pastorella*. Here the poet-narrator, straying in the woods, stumbles upon a girl who seems half-shepherdess, half-nymph. The girl says that when she hears the song of birds, she wants a lover and, quite magically, the birds start singing. There follows a delightful interlude, which ends in Pound's translation:

> She held to me with a dear willfulness
> Saying her heart had gone into my bosom,
> She drew me on to a cool leafy place
> Where I gat sight of every coloured blossom,
> And there I drank in so much summer sweetness
> Meseemed Love's god connived at its completeness.

There is no doubt that the romantic vision ends in a sexual act. This is not phantasy for the sake of phantasy. One has both the realistic act and the vision to contain it. After his translation of the *Donna mi prega* in Canto 36, Pound includes the line "Sacrum, sacrum, in-luminatio coitu" (Holy, holy the illumination in coitus). Guido, Pound felt, supplied both the romance necessary to cover the act with dignity, and also a frank awareness of its necessity. Thus Pound uses the simplest pastourelles of Cavalcanti to convey a sense of the mystical metaphysics of sexual energy. Most Cavalcanti commentators would say that he reads too much into the poetry, but none of them is able to add anything convincing about that river full of lamias; nor is anyone fully capable of explaining a phrase like *tondo sesto* (changed by Pound to *tondo di Sesto)* in Sonnet XIV (p. 52).[6] Pound's insights, which are those of a poet, often are far more suggestive than other people's prose suppositions.

The second phase of Guido's work might be called the Platonic period. It includes some poems in which Guido is very clearly using the correspondences of a metaphysical structure in a way that aligns him with Guinizelli and the later Dante. The most striking is Sonnet XXXV, which is addressed to Guido Orlando, and in which, as Pound puts it in the epigraph: "He explains the miracles of the madonna of Or San Michele, by telling whose image it is" *(Trans.,* pp. 94 f.). In this poem Guido equates his own *donna* with Madonna, just as Dante formed the Beatrice-Christ parallel in *Vita Nuova* XXIV, but the monks in the poem call the poet a pagan:

> Great ills she cureth in an open place,
> With reverence the folk all kneel unto her,
> And two lamps shed the glow about her form.
>
> Her voice is borne out through far-lying ways
> 'Till brothers minor cry: 'Idolatry,'
> For envy of her precious neighborhood.

This poem is cited in Canto 4/16:18, where Guido's woman is merged with a painting of the Madonna in Ortolo by Stefano da Verona (the names Ortolo and Orsanmichele coalescing):

> Adige, thin film of images,
> Across the Adige, by Stefano, Madonna in hortulo,
> As Cavalcanti had seen her.

Cavalcanti and Stefano—two makers—blend together, as do the artistic cities of Verona and Florence and the Rivers Arno and Adige.

Pound rightfully holds up Sonnet VII (pp. 38 f.) as one of Guido's finest performances, belaboring previous editors such as Arnone for adopting inferior readings in the second line:[7]

> Who is she that comes, makyng turn every man's eye
> And makyng the air to tremble with a bright clearenesse

That leadeth with her Love, in such nearness
No man may proffer of speech more than a sigh?

Chi è questa che vien, ch'ogni uom la mira,
Che fa di clarità l'aer tremare,
E mena seco Amor, sí che parlare
Null'uom ne puote, ma ciascún sospira?

The much-debated second line becomes important to Pound not only for its metaphysical vibrations, but also for the war he waged against academicians to preserve its beauty. He includes it in Canto 74/448:476, where it blends with Romanesque forms in Verona:

veder Nap'oiiiii or Pavia the romanesque
                being preferable
and by analogy the form of San Zeno the
        columns signed by their maker
            the frescoes in S. Pietro and the madonna in Ortolo
e "fa di clarità l'aer tremare"
as in the manuscript of the Capitolare

The third phase of Cavalcanti is that admired by Joyce's Stephen Daedalus as Guido of "the dark humor."[8] Here we find the anti-papal, darkly tragic, psychologically oriented poet who sings more about Amor's bitter arrows and the tears of love than about its transcendent possibilities. Pound catches this side of Guido very well, as in Ballata XII (pp. 124 ff.), when he translates:

Love that is born of loving like delight,
Within my heart sojourneth
And fashions a new person from desire
Yet toppleth down to vileness all his might. . .

Amor, che nasce di simil piacere,
Dentro da'l cor si posa,
Formando di desio nova persona,
Ma fa la sua virtù 'n vizio cadere. . .

At first the tone sounds uplifted and optimistic. Yet this mood dissolves as virtue descends to vice. Pound uses the third line in a similarly dramatic way to open Canto 27, but the Italian is quickly followed by "One man is dead, and another has rotted his end off." The Cavalcanti verse is an ideal against which the vicious particulars of World War I are measured.

Before turning to Guido's masterwork, let us say that Pound was fully aware of the two Guidos of lyric: the transcendental mystic and the empirical psychologist. This awareness may account for his twofold handling of the *Donna mi prega*, a poem that we must consider in some detail because of the emphasis that Pound places on it in his epic.

❊ ❊ ❊ ❊

The *Donna mi prega* or so-called *Canzone d'amore* (Song of Love), which appears in Pound's final translation in Canto 36, was written to define love in response to a sonnet by Guido Orlandi *(Lit. Essays,* p. 199), who had posed various questions. In discussing the Italian, I shall use the already cited text of Giulio Cattaneo. Pound's text, which appears among other places in *Literary Essays* (pp. 163 ff.), was primarily based on his own reading of the Laurentian manuscript Pl. XL, 46, with consultation of the Bernardo da Giunta edition of 1527. The manuscript is not highly regarded by scholars, but Pound selected it deliberately since he thought it was free of tampering from the Church.

Almost everyone, including Pound, believes that the finest early commentary is that of the physician Dino del Garbo, who died in 1327.[9] Similarly almost everyone condemns the commentary attributed to Egidio Colonna, now called the work of the Pseudo-Colonna, because of its philosophical naiveté.[10] Dino the Doctor was a man with a strongly empirical bent that Pound found very congenial. Dino tends to treat the poem in psychological and physiological terms, looking upon the love described in an almost pathological sense; he uses Aristotle and various Arabic thinkers as his primary sources. During the Renaissance commentators like Paolo del Rosso tended to treat the poem in an opposite way, as totally Neoplatonic.[11] After the Age of Reason, which saw little to admire in anything medieval, Guido was revived in the nineteenth century, first by Romantics looking for an Italian past with anticlerical heroes (Carducci, Arnone), and finally by specialized commentators like Giulio Salvadori and Karl Vossler.[12] Both of the latter pointed out the Arabic qualities in Guido's thought, and this general direction was fully implemented with the fine scholarship of the Italian critic Bruno Nardi, upon whose work I shall be quite dependent.[13]

An opposing modern critic was J. E. Shaw, who stoutly denied that the poem was essentially Averroistic, pointing out that it was neither more nor less dependent on Arabic thought than was the work of Albertus Magnus, one of the pillars of the Christian Church.[14] Shaw used Albertus for almost all of his documentations, and indeed the learned saint goes a long way toward explicating some of the difficult phrases of the poem. In the process, Guido emerges sounding very orthodox. Gone is the daring vigor that Pound sensed in the language. Nardi summarized the basic nature of Cavalcanti's work in voicing the following critique of Shaw:

> If the love Cavalcanti treats is the contemplation of an idea, how can one explain that pessimism that pervades all of Cavalcanti's lyrics and that leads the poet to represent the passion of love as an obfuscation of reason and a cause for twisting man away from 'the perfect good'?   (*SD, 25,* 1940, 51)

This remark vindicates Pound's long and tireless labor to resuscitate Guido—a labor that Shaw almost totally dismissed. Still, Shaw's attitude toward Pound was not universally shared, for Otto Bird, the editor of Del Garbo, cooperated with Pound in the thirties and freely expressed his gratitude to the poet.[15]

The ironic fact is that after the time of Emperor Frederick II (who is with Guido's father in Dante's Circle of Heretics) almost everyone was to some degree drawn to the man-oriented line of Averroistic thought, a philosophy that saw the Possible Intellect in man in touch with that eternal Mind that governs the universe, but which also treated it as something split, cut off, glimmering beautifully but solitarily in a world surrounded by dark and destructive matter. There is no Platonic comedy in Averroes' world, no comedic union with a perpetual figure. The comforting worlds of Platonic ideas and Christian angels are dismissed, and man finds himself caught in a perplexing tension between body and soul. We have already seen this dilemma expressed in phase three of Cavalcanti's lyrics.

The first stanza of the *Donna mi prega* establishes the methodology of the work: it will proceed by "natural demonstration"—not by recourse to authority, divine revelation, or intuition. Guido states in the second line that love is an *accidente* (an accident in the Scholastic sense, or, as Pound translates it, an "affect"). Del Garbo stresses the Aristotelian distinction being made here: love is not a substance (and therefore, perhaps, a god), but is instead a movement within a substance, like an appetite or a passion such as ire, fear, or sadness. From the start we see that Guido is adopting the language of a scientist who wants to prove *(voler provare)* a point.

In the second stanza we find that the poem will divide into two parts. We shall hear about the first perfection of love, its creation; ensuing stanzas will deal with its second perfection, its operation. The stanza dealing with love's creation sounds very Neoplatonic:

> Where memory liveth,
>   it takes its state
> Formed like a diafan from light on shade
> Which shadow cometh of Mars and remaineth
> Created, having a name sensate,
> Custom of the soul,
>   will from the heart. . .

> *In quella parte—dove sta memora*
> *prende suo stato,—sí formato,—come*
> *diaffan da lume,—d'una scuritate*
>   *la qual da Marte—vène, e fa demora;*
> *elli è creato—ed ha sensato—nome,*
> *d'alma costume—e di cor volontate.*

But the terminology is also Aristotelian. Guido is saying that love establishes itself in the place where memory is. This is, as Shaw points out, the sensitive part of the soul or the interior senses: "having a name sensate."[16] The stress here is entirely upon the connection between memory and the senses in the Aristotelian-Scholastic tradition; it is opposed to the Augustinian tradition, which saw the soul as a composition of memory, intelligence, and will, with the emphasis on the latter.

The sixth line of the stanza makes a distinction clear: love derives its habitual modus from the soul ("custom of the soul"), the entire being of the body, and is therefore naturally allied to some extent with intellect and reason (as opposed to the beasts), but it takes its will or direction from the heart, a physical organ that draws the action into the realm of the senses. Here is the nexus of the problem: the cleft between ideal function and actual operation. Yet love is also connected with the formation of light out of darkness. Pound uses this line to link Guido directly to the Neoplatonic tradition, and Shaw does the same, interpreting Guido's *lume* as that "light of the First Cause, the 'Intellectus universaliter agens' which itself is pure light.

It creates everything and illuminates everything in the universe."[17]
Nardi rails out at this tendency to make everything so comfortable,
pointing up the allusion to Mars, whose influence is usually malign.[18]
It is true that the dark element is the abiding one *(fa demora)*, and this
statement sounds ominous. There is light without first-hand illumination. Nardi seems to have hit on the right tone, even though Pound's
suggestion that the Martian influence can be interpreted by "impulse" makes the astronomical imagery work more dramatically.[19]

Pound uses the line about memory in Canto 63/353:370 to describe John Adams' activities:

Read one book an hour
            then dine, smoke, cut wood
                                        in quella parte
dove sta memora, Colonel Chandler not conscious
these crude thoughts and expressions
are catched up and treasured as proof of his character.

Here we have Adams nurturing his mind, acquainting himself with a
vast body of facts and abstracting the basic forms that he will use to
help forge America. The contrasting figure does not know how to use
these "crude thoughts and expressions," these *phantasmata.* Later
in the *Pisan Cantos,* when Pound is denied books and must depend on
his memory, he returns to that sensitive part of the inner self to
summon up the ghosts of the past:

            nothing matters but the quality
of the affection—
in the end—that has carved the trace in the mind
dove sta memoria.   (Canto 76/457:485)

The Cavalcanti tagline underscores the sensitive, almost sentimental
nature of memory, as opposed to the dry, intellective way in which
other philosophers might use the term.

The word *diaffan* is also important. In Albertus Magnus' *De
anima,* or commentary on Aristotle's *Peri psyches,* we find the following definition: "For we see light not by itself but in a certain
subject, and this is the diafane."[20] The emphasis here is not on
metaphysics, but on the actual process of vision; and the part that a
visible body, *subiecto,* plays is important. Pound's poetic use of the
notion far surpasses the mere philosophical statement. Whether Plato

or Aristotle is in the back of his mind is unimportant, for in Canto 93/632:665, we see the formation of an ideal in act:

> You are tender as a marshmallow, my Love,
> I cannot use you as a fulcrum.
> > You have stirred my mind out of dust.
> Flora Castalia, your petals drift thru the air,
> the wind is ½ lighted with pollen
> > > > diafana,
> e Monna Vanna . . . tu mi fai rimembrar.   *(you make me remember)*

The effect here is truly metamorphic in an Ovidian sense, for we have events from the natural world (drifting pollen, the round soft whiteness of marshmallow) suggesting a blurred world in which actual forms merge with ideals: a mythical flower goddess, Flora, blends with the fountain of Castalia, where she might well be sitting; Cavalcanti's woman, Giovanna or Lady Vanna, is placed there, along with Cavalcanti's philosophical but highly imagistic word "diafana." To complete the picture, we have an echo of the lovely line from Dante's *Purgatorio* XXVIII.49, when Dante sees the nymph Matelda sitting on a bank in the Earthly Paradise atop Mount Purgatory. He thinks about that nymph of old, Proserpina, who was raped by Pluto and thus caused the dissolution of a beautifully delicate world of light, grace, and the senses in the Vale of Enna. Magically all of these things coalesce around the Cavalcanti touchstones.

The last half of the second stanza of Guido's poem describes the creation of an ambience for love, which is really the formation of an ideal (with emphasis on the Greek verb *idein*, to see, not to conjecture idly or to mull abstractly):

> Cometh from a seen form which being understood
> Taketh locus and remaining in the intellect possible
> Wherein hath he neither weight nor still-standing,
> Descendeth not by quality but shineth out
> Himself his own effect unendingly
> Not in delight but in the being aware
> Nor can he leave his true likeness otherwise.

> *Vèn da veduta forma che s'intende,*
> *che prende—nel possibile intelletto,*

come in subietto,–loco e dimoranza,
In quella parte mai non ha possanza
* perché da qualitate non descende:*
resplende–in sé perpetüal effetto;
non ha diletto–ma consideranza;
sí che non pote largir simiglianza.

Pound gives a precise, straightforward, but highly abbreviated version of this difficult passage. With reference to the Italian text of Cattaneo-Favati, Cavalcanti is saying here that a beautiful figure, a seen form *(veduta forma),* is understood *(s'intende)* or encompassed by the sensitive part of the soul, which then transfers this vision to the Possible Intellect, where it is kept in a kind of permanent storage, having a fixed place *(loco)* and a long period of abiding *(dimoranza).* There inside the Possible Intellect, it stands as a subject, and therefore has no—great textual problem here—*possanza* (potency) or *posanza* (restfulness) or *pesanza* (weight or sadness). Shaw takes Casella's reading of *pesanza,* but I concur with Pound that this is simplistic, since later Cavalcanti says that there is no joy here; why would he also want to stress the absence of sadness? The Possible Intellect is that storagehouse for meditation that is beyond the immediate reach of the senses, and is in fact in touch with the divine ideals, according to St. Albert and others.[21] Pound blends two of the three possible readings for the word into one line when he says that there is neither weight nor true repose ("still-standing") here. This is a brave attempt, and perhaps not wrong, but the solution of Favati-Cattaneo with the reading *possanza* makes better sense. The idealized form has no *potency,* cannot move, precisely because, as Guido goes on to say, it cannot descend through qualities or down into qualities. It can only stay in the mind and shine *(resplende),* a perpetual effect because it is in touch with divinely enduring Ideal Beauty. It has no pleasure *(diletto* in Guido) except that of *consideranza,* which Shaw calls reflection (p. 48).

Although many critics would quarrel with Pound's interpretations, his poetic uses of the above material lie beyond dispute. For example, he employs the bare word *risplende* (in his text) to convey a sense of the shining eyes of goddesses and beautiful women who act as perpetual ideals, beaming into the phenomenal world as seen actualities, not as abstractions:

> To Queen Nephertari this incense
>   To Isis this incense
>   "quest' unire
> "quale è dentro l'anima
>   veggendo di fuori quelli che ama"
>   Risplende
> From the sea-caves
>   degli occhi
> Manifest and not abstract.   (Canto 93/625:658)

The words inside the quotation marks, taken from *Convivio* III.ii.9, merely underscore what is said in the Cavalcanti poem: "this union takes place inside the soul, seeing what it loves outside."

In the third stanza, having established the creation of ideals, Guido now shows love in act. The opening lines are difficult because the words *vertute* and *perfezione* are ambiguous:

> He is not vertu but cometh of that perfection
> Which is so postulate not by the reason
> But 'tis felt, I say.

> *Non è vertute,–ma da quella vène*
> *ch'è perfezione–(ché si pone–tale),*
> *non razionale,–ma che sente, dico.*

Shaw prefers to translate both words in moral terms: "Love is not a moral virtue but is derived from that faculty (technically called *virtue*) which is sensitive, and not from the rational faculty" (p. 52). However, this reading raises certain questions, as Nardi pointed out: "If love is a passion, this cannot come from a moral virtue, because the moral virtues rein in the passions, and do not spur them on."[22] Nardi asks further, "How can a moral virtue be a perfection, and yet not be rational?" as the third line emphasizes. Nardi goes on to read the passage as follows, aligning the words with Averroistic doctrine: "Love is not a *virtù* or faculty of the soul, but a passion that comes from that virtue or faculty which is a perfection (that is, the form of a human body) . . . either from the sensitive virtue or faculty, but not from the intellectual virtue or faculty."

The third line above haunted Pound. He uses it to great advantage in Canto 67/391:411, when John Adams is meditating as follows:

honour is a mere fragment of virtue, yet sacred . . .
foundation of every government in some principle
or passion of the people
            ma che si sente dicho
Locke Milton Nedham Neville Burnet and Hoadly
empire of laws not of men

Pound is saying here through Adams that ideals cannot be put
into action without the appropriate sentiment to accompany them.
The rule of a benevolent Chinese despot like Yong Tching in Canto 61
is far more effective than the formal thought of a Locke or the frigid
aesthetics of the Puritan Milton. Pound is fond of pointing out the
heart radical in Chinese ideograms, as well as what he calls the biceps
or muscle element to indicate strength of will. He tends to merge, as
Guido does, the intellect of the soul with the heart, the emotions.

In the next few lines Cavalcanti seems to be talking like a
twentieth-century psychologist, for he speaks of love almost as the
impulse toward a thing, without any consideration of whether it is
good or bad. Reason is now totally at the mercy of the phantasmata,
which issue from the mind, and the passions, which emanate from the
senses:

Beyond salvation, holdeth his judging force
Deeming intention to be reason's peer and mate,
Poor in discernment, being thus weakness' friend
Often his power cometh on death in the end . . .

    for di salute–giudicar mantene,
ché la 'ntenzione–per ragione–vale:
discerne male–in cui è vizio amico.
    Di sua potenza segue spesso morte . . .

Albertus Magnus says in the *De anima* III.4.vi (p. 235) that an
intellect unmixed with phantasmata "is always and entirely right";
however, "phantasy and the appetites are right and not right." It all
depends on whether one has the *intentionem boni*, "intention toward
the good," Guido's *intenzione*. My own neutral translation of the last
part of this stanza reads:

But by how far from the Perfect Good it is twisted
Through chance, by that far does a man not have life,
For stability no longer has its mastery.
And a similar thing occurs when a man forgets it (puts love aside).

ma quanto che da buon perfetto tort'è
per sorte,–non pò dire om ch'aggia vita,
ché stabilita–non ha segnoria.
A simil pò valer quand'om l'oblia.

Love as appetite (Aristotle's *orexis*), as physical function, is thus clearly acknowledged (and not frowned upon, à la St. Augustine); but love as a part of the soul, and therefore not totally removed from the intellective virtues, is also insisted upon. When Guido says that love can lead to death, I think he means just that: physical death, not just the "death in life" that he often sings about in his sonnets. I would even go so far as to claim that there is a sexual pun here, for the word *morto* still in modern Italian means "flaccid, spent in sex," and I believe that there is the sense here that through the actualization of its potency *(potenza,* another word with sexual possibilities), love can lead to that state of physical exhaustion which is a sign of general flaccidity. Eliot's hollow men in *The Waste Land* are morally, mentally, and physically exhausted; they do not, in the words of Guido's beautiful *Perch' i' no spero di tornar giammai,* "hope to turn again."

Stanzas four and five come as something of a relief after what has gone before, for here we have the effects of love portrayed, and the difficulties are more textual than contextual. Here is described the agony of love, the so-called *passio ereos* that is found in Chaucer, the *Roman de la rose,* the troubadours, and was described most fully by the Moslem doctor Avicenna. Pound's translation of this section in Canto 36 conveys most of the accepted meanings. His notes on the word *ira* and his translation of it as "uneasiness" are extremely perceptive and fully in accord with late medieval Aristotelian expression.[23] Still, there are some rough places. Pound insists on reading "Willing man look into that forméd trace in his mind" for line 51, when the manuscripts yield either *non formato* (not formed) or *non fermato* (unclosed), instead of *un formato.* Pound here wants to return to the first perfection of love and talk about those traces formed in the memory which abide through a man's life, but the line is hardly that grand; it seems to be doing little more than to revoice the old maxim about lovers standing and staring idly into unformed or formless space. Another objection can be raised about the word *bianco* in line 64, which Pound renders "taken in the white light that is allness." Guido actually seems to be saying that "white fails or falls in such an object" (that is, the *viso* or face of the lover in the preceding line). The meaning is simply that a lover's face is pale and colorless.

At the poem's end, Cavalcanti describes love for a final time, as Pound translates in Canto 36:

Being divided, set out from colour,
Disjunct in mid darkness
Grazeth the light, one moving by other,
Being divided, divided from all falsity
Worthy of trust[24]
From him alone mercy proceedeth.

For di colore, d'essere diviso,
assiso-'n mezzo scuro, luce rade.
For d'ogne fraude–dico, degno in fede,
che solo di costui nasce mercede.

These lines harken back to stanza 2, where light was pictured as a diaphanous phenomenon shrouding the black medium of matter. After his very precise, physiological description of the workings of love, Cavalcanti returns to his suggestion that love is in some remote way linked to the First Cause and the intellectual light of the spheres. Thus the door is once again open to Neoplatonic interpretations.

I have expended a great deal of space in my exegesis of the poem to show how accurate Pound often was in his translating, despite his carping critics. Whenever he diverges from the text, as in the last stanza, where he truncates severely, we should ask ourselves why. I believe that the answer is fairly obvious. Pound wants to eliminate any parts of Guido's psychology that verge upon Scholastic thought and away from Neoplatonic light theory. Therefore he omits one whole phrase in line 48 *(poco soggiorna:* "lasts but a little") in his attempt to suppress Guido's insistence on the brevity of love, and he ignores line 56, which says that love bestows "no great wisdom nor small." Similarly, "Being divided" in the lines above does not adequately render the Italian, which says "divided from being"—a condition that is much more ominous.

Let me state the case more specifically. Nardi has proved to the satisfaction of most Cavalcanti theorists that Guido is an Averroist skeptic who does not believe in life after death, in union with the Agent Intellect, or in any of the other comforting ideas of his day. Pound admires the man's Aristotelian preciseness in attitude, but when it comes to a full interpretation of Guido's doctrine of love, he attempts to steer him into the camp of Scotus and Richard of St.

Victor, and away from Albertus Magnus, Thomas Aquinas, and the other syllogizers. As a scholar, Pound might be criticized, but as a poet, he is free to adapt as he pleases. Whether one agrees with Pound's interpretation of the philosophy is ultimately unimportant, for the scientific Guido who emerges from Canto 36 *sings* in ways that he never does in the contradictory commentaries written about him. As for his own connection with Guido, Pound, like Dante, tended to eventually put him aside. In his youth and crusading middle years, Pound found the lonely skeptic with the clinical eye enormously fascinating, but as he grew older, Pound rediscovered the more enduring effect of Dante. We shall explore this further in Chapter 8, when we consider the epic poetry written in this period. As for the general question of ideals and reality, of Plato and Aristotle, of Scholasticism and Neoplatonism—ultimately one finds that it is difficult to include one member to the exclusion of its opposite. The general frameworks of both the *Comedy* and the *Cantos* are idealistic, mystical, and visionary; the executions of the works are precise, empirical, practical. Cavalcanti could be used in developing the methodology of the work, but when it came to root ideas, Guido finally had to yield to Alighieri.

6

THE MIDDLE PHASE: MONARCHY AND MONEY

We have already noted, in discussing the lives of the two poets, the ways in which their middle years were occupied with political concerns. In Dante's case, the period from about 1295 to 1313 is concerned with the politics of the Holy Roman Empire, and the latter part of that with the figure of Henry VII. In the period from 1920 to 1945, Pound was drawn to the reforms he saw effected in Fascism, showing also a deep concern with monetary issues. Once again we find that our poets have a strong common bond, in that they are not in any sense mere "aesthetes." In fact, it may even be conjectured that Dante's extensive writings on politics and philosophy colored Pound's own views on the same subjects to some extent.

Unfortunately, the *De monarchia*, in which Dante expresses the nexus of his political beliefs, does not fall properly into the period delineated above, despite Boccaccio's suggestion that it does.[1] In Book I.xii.6 of his work, Dante makes a random comment about a passage that he had written in the *Paradiso,* and since we cannot believe that he would have written that last part of his masterwork early in his career, we are forced to date the *De monarchia* close to the author's death. But an exact date is unimportant, for the ideas expressed in the treatise are the same ones that we saw voiced in the letters quoted in Chapter 1. Dante was strongly and passionately on the side of the Emperor as opposed to the Pope in the arena of human affairs. He called for an absolute split between secular and ecclesiastical power, seeing the end of man as double *(duplex finis,* III.xv.6), with both an earthly and a heavenly fulfillment, and not, as the Church viewed it, with the celestial taking precedence over the terrestrial. In a word, he fought for the Earthly Paradise.

The *De monarchia* itself is more interesting for its ideas than for its methodology.[2] The work is full of slipshod syllogisms; in fact, some of the reasoning is so faulty and tenuous that one begins to see why Pound attacked the logical form so violently.[3] Too much is assumed, for one thing, in the major premise; thus the entire argumentation is slanted from the start. There are also questionable analogies, tedious appeals to authority (shades of Scotus Erigena!), and numerous *ad hominem* allusions, especially to Aristotle. Since the opposition was indulging in the same practices, however, Dante can be excused; he was, as Pound always regarded him, very much a child of his age. Still, there is a great power and integrity in the work, one that humanistic scholars like De Sanctis and Vossler have readily acknowledged.[4] For example, Dante's definition of Justice in I.xi as Will and Power directed by Love is one that accords with Pound's own notions on the subject, backed by Chinese ideograms and expressed in the Latin term *directio voluntatis*.[5]

Dante was fighting entrenched bigotry, trying to rise above petty politics, trying to establish a Reich that would in some way recall the grandeur of Rome. German muscle and the Latin past are as important to him as they became for Pound, who was forced to rely on Hitler as the real power behind Mussolini, and who always saw the Roman Empire as a great European achievement. We therefore tend to read the *De monarchia* with mixed feelings. We applaud the intention, even if we decry the means of achieving it. In Book I when Dante is trying to prove the necessity of the Empire, he uses many of the traditional arguments for monistic proofs of God, such as those popularized by Boethius in his *Consolation of Philosophy*. However, in Book III when he is debating whether a man needs an intermediary between himself and God, he reverses his attack and adopts a dualistic approach that subverts the previous monistic position. Actually, the arguments used in Book I could be used by the opposition in Book III (and, in fact, they were, in the bulls of Boniface VIII), but Dante ignores the possibility.

Indeed, if we summon up the ghost of the much-cited Aristotle, and if we read his *Nicomachean Ethics* with the care that Pound devoted to the task in *Kulchur* (pp. 304 ff.), we see how utterly misleading the argumentation can be. One could substitute the word "tyranny" for "monarchy" at almost every juncture. For isn't the power that Dante is so willing to hand over to one man in an unchecked way often the very source of evil? John Adams saw this, as he said in a letter to Thomas Jefferson, cited in Canto 69: "You fear the one, I the few." But Dante, living in chaotic Italy, with the Church swept into French captivity in Avignon, was willing to thrust power into the hands of anyone who was able to bring some order into the situation. Similarly, Pound wanted to fall back on Mussolini to cut through the notorious Italian bureaucratic process in order to put Italy back on its feet. Yet the reversion of monarchy to despotism is one that Aristotle was keenly aware of when he said that if things go wrong, monarchies are the worst form of government. The truth of the proposition is proved in Pound's Chinese Cantos. To Dante's credit, we must acknowledge the brilliant vindication of Imperial Rome in Book II, which is answered by Pound's palinode ROMA—AMOR.[6] And we must acknowledge the modernity of his aim (which is really the creation of a United Europe of sorts), as well as the humanitarian drive of his purpose.

Since Dante is obsessed with social issues and political aims, we may find it strange that there is no ideal city in the *Divine Comedy*, just as there is no hero in the traditional epic sense. In Hell, there is a noble castle of philosophers in a very medieval setting (meant to recall the Grove of Academe); and there is a wicked City of Dis for the heretics; but the rest of the sinners are alone, cut off; there is no city because there is none of the order which is necessary to create one. On Mount Purgatory, there is likewise no community proper, for the place is divided into a succession of rounds, and everyone is concerned with his own salvation. The people sing and undergo ritual acts together, but these are not, properly speaking, the activities of a city; they are the rites of a temple. At the top of the mountain we have what Dante calls his Earthly Paradise; to Pound, this would be the City of Dioce or the perfect community, but to Dante it is a garden which harkens back to Eden and to the other rural places of pastoral romance. Paradise proper to Dante is the outward-going cosmos, where the individual gradually loses his personality and becomes a part of pure form; here the notion of the human community is transcended, rather than realized. The presence of an urban sense is a basic difference between Dante and Pound, and perhaps between the medieval mind and the modern. As for the heroes? Most of the traditional figures are in Hell: Tristan, Julius Caesar, Augustus Caesar, Frederick II, Alexander the Great. We have Charlemagne in Heaven, along with other warriors of God, but the heroic to Dante was an extremely questionable value. He had seen too much blood and gore to want to write another *Song of Roland;* he was too much of a realist to put his faith ultimately in any one man; his Greyhound is impersonal. As a realist, he did the sensible thing: seeing no man to glorify, he made himself the center of his song, just as Pound in the anti-heroic twentieth century did. Let us say that in both writers Mind takes precedence over Muscle, and that is perhaps what The Epic of Judgement really means in comparison with other exemplars of the epic form. The protagonist in both poems is an intellectual seeking pragmatic truths in a metaphysical ambience. Both writers are classicists; both are anti-romantic, as we see when we compare Dante with Chrétien de Troyes and Wolfram von Eschenbach. Although a city is lacking as a setting in the *Comedy,* how that work resounds with political talk! Everyone seems to want to know what is going on back in his native city or state. We have the current events of Romany and Lombardy and Tuscany recited for us, just as in the *Cantos* we have long rolls of the good kings of Anglo-Saxon England and the emperors of Byzantium. Pound and Dante both dote upon specific factual detail, almost as if there was magic in the incantation of a name.

Furthermore, in the *Comedy* Dante frequently mentions money, thus endearing himself even more to his successor. When Sordello castigates the Earthly Princes in the vale upon the mountain in *Purgatorio* VII.73, gold and refined silver are mentioned as norms by which to judge the natural beauty of the place. Pound was always aware of the great emphasis that Dante placed upon money.[7] He noted, for example, that the sins which arise from sensual excess are treated more lightly. than those which stem from intentional fraud (misdirection of the *directio voluntatis*). Sexual sinners like Paolo and Francesca in *Inferno* V are put well above the disgusting counterfeiters in Canto XXX. The lovable glutton Ciacco of Canto VI is treated less harshly than are the degraded sellers of public and ecclesiastical offices in Cantos XIX and XXI. These ideas accorded perfectly with Pound's economic theories, and they fit with those of the monetary expert Alexander del Mar. Del Mar, like Pound, believed that the world underwent a dangerous and critical shift in the late seventeenth century: first, the excesses of the Puritan Revolution, followed by the opposite excesses of the Restoration; he thought that sexual crimes became the obsessions of religious leaders who at the same time were opening the door to usurers and other exploiters of nature.[8] Pound insists upon the value of sex in Cantos 20 and 39 with an anti-puritanical vengeance. Similarly Dante, for his own age, was extremely tolerant. He faints upon seeing Paolo and Francesca. He treats the homosexual Brunetto Latini with loving care in *Inferno* XV. Even the whores and the pimps of *Inferno* XVIII, who reduce love to commerce, are in the highest ditch of their perverted world of the eighth circle. Dante may not make economics the center of his work as Pound does, but he is certainly sensitive to its importance. When the noble homosexuals ask him what is wrong in Florence, he replies: "the *nouveaux riches* and the quick buck" *(La gente nuova e i subiti guadagni, Inf.* XVI.73).

Pound's coupling of economics and literature is not difficult to relate. From the publication of *A Lume Spento* in 1908, he was determined to write an epic, as he showed in the poem "Scriptor Ignotus." He later decided to define that genre as follows: "An epic is a poem including history. I don't see that anyone save a sap-head can now think he knows any history until he understands economics."[9] The important influence in his London years was A. R. Orage, who employed Ezra to write many articles on music and books for his journal, the *New Age*. At these offices in 1918, when Pound was destitute, he met Major C. H. Douglas, who was working on the so-called Social Credit theory, which sought to replace wages and salaries with shares of business in the hope of reducing the inequities created by industries, which constantly raise their prices because they demand more money to work than they release.[10] In addition, Pound was attracted to the work of the German economist Silvio Gesell, who believed that inflation could be rectified by the use of the *Schwundgeld* or the Demurrage Money system, through which money would bear coupons which, if not used, would diminish the value of the paper to which they were attached.[11]

As Pound showed in the 1952 addendum to *Kulchur* (p. 352), another important influence was Brooks Adams, especially for his *Law of Civilization and Decay*.[12] This work, following Vico, looked at history in a cyclical way, and, like Marx, from an economic viewpoint. To read Adams is to see cultures waxing and waning like organisms under microscopes. This is precisely the feeling that one gets from the first thirty *Cantos,* where we see the Renaissance swelling under the impact of a good leader like Sigismundo Malatesta and declining under the corrupt Borgias. Pound learned many things from Adams—when he finally discovered him in the 1940's—some things which corroborated Pound's own suppositions drawn purely from art. Adams' final chapter, in fact, relates architecture to history and money in an ideogrammic way. Ezra also indulged in some of Brooks' prejudices: a touch of antisemitism; a tendency to ignore Charlemagne; an early despisal of Byzantines as an "ostentatious, sordid, cowardly, and stagnant race," although each of these excesses was rectified later.[13]

Pound moved from Paris to Italy in the 1920's because he wanted to see theories transformed into acts. Mussolini made Pound feel that here at last was a ruler who was capable of instituting economic reforms, who could bring labor into a strong role in his corporate state, and who was employing intelligent men like Delcroix, Por, and Rossoni to execute his ideas. During the 1930's Pound wrote his *ABC of Economics* and several Money Pamphlets; his ideas on economics are most accessible in the later published *Impact.* When Mussolini fell, Pound was forced to revert to his abstract ideals; thereafter in the *Cantos* he shows no enthusiasm for any savior in the flesh.

During the confinement at St. Elizabeths, Pound stumbled upon the almost unknown Alexander del Mar. This man, the Director of the Bureau of Statistics in Washington in the late nineteenth century, had access to all of the government records relating to money and exchange. Del Mar proceeded to study economics closely and wrote a series of books propounding his theories which, as expressed in *The Science of Money,* can be grossly simplified as follows: 1) money is a measure, not a thing, and as such does not and should not be tied to one commodity, such as gold, which can then be regulated by speculators; 2) money must be measured and regulated by the state (indeed, that is the state's prime function); it should not abrogate this right to others, especially to private individuals, as it has done in most countries; 3) money as the life-blood of a state must be measured primarily in terms of that state; it does not need recourse to outside organisms (this fact is proved by the economic life of Soviet Russia).

Del Mar, like many of Pound's discoveries, is a brilliant stylist with a gift for precise definition: "Exchange is a social act: no man can exchange with himself."[14] His allusions to the arts are cogent and informative. His zeal for reform was great, for he felt, as did Pound, that the money of the world had fallen into the hands of monetary speculators (Pound's usurocrats and the "gnomes of Zurich" of the daily newspapers), who could raise the German mark or sink the British pound at their will.

Del Mar's views of history also coincided with Pound's. He admired those periods in the histories of China and Rome when the empires had regulated their coinage for the good of all citizens. Del Mar also believed, like Adams and Pound, that something went wrong in the late Renaissance. Del Mar dated the event precisely in 1666, when King Charles II of England, at the prompting of his mistress Barbara Villiers and through the action of the Dutch East Indies Company, abrogated his royal right to regulate the coin and turned the mint over to the hands of private coiners, thereby creating that mysterious figure known as The Modern Financier, Pound's Usurocrat, cast in the shadow of Dante's monster Geryon.[15]

Del Mar differs from the early Pound radically in two major respects: 1) he is not the slightest bit antisemitic; his *Usury and the Jews* is a very fair assessment of the way in which Jews were *forced* in the Middle Ages to assume the role of money-lending because they were denied the land; even when treating the Rothschilds, whose malign influence he records, he does not generalize; 2) he treats Charlemagne as a cruel and somewhat ignorant tyrant, not as benevolent despot, the way Pound ultimately sees him.[17] Del Mar is perhaps most interesting because of his tone, for although the statistician-historian is grievously troubled by the contemporary state of economics, he never voices rabid denunciations.

Pound, like Dante, is impetuous. It was remarked in Chapter 1 that Pound during his years at Rapallo became increasingly bitter in the tone of his writing. Although he always swore that he did not want a "Kaisertum uberalles,"[18] in the book *Jefferson and/or Mussolini* he is clearly on the side of the Italian. *Kulchur* purports to establish an ideogrammic method that will bring together all of the aspects of a culture, presumably for the purposes of study and without regard for definite judgements. But it is clear from the chapter labeled "Totalitarian" and from many statements inside that the book is the work of a confirmed monist. Indeed, Pound seems to have reached his political ideas through philosophy. Having adopted a form of Neoplatonism with a strong emphasis on Plotinus, Porphyry, and Scotus Erigena, he then seems to have gradually succumbed to the monistic assumption of the political within the theological. Ardent Poundians will of course contend that the *Cantos* are written with Aristotelian fairness, that they do not insist upon the establishment of a dynasty simply because they describe one. Does Pound not, after all, make the founding of the American democracy the single most significant event in the modern history of the tribe? Yes. But during his middle years, which we are primarily concerned with here, there is no concealing a great yearning on Pound's part for a benevolent despot, for a Sigismundo, a Tai Tsong, an Athelstan, a Justinian, a Trajan, a Mussolini. In the 1930's, Pound was every bit as monistic as Dante, for he stood firmly on the side of The One.

7

TWO VIEWS OF HELL: THE INFERNAL AND THE EPHEMERAL

Returning to the guidelines for epic construction that we established in Chapter 3, we are now ready to focus upon the first triads of our writers' masterworks. We shall lay the *Inferno* next to the Early Cantos, the *Purgatorio* next to the Middle Cantos and the *Paradiso* beside the Later Cantos. In proceeding thus, we do not expect the differing segments to accord, for as I stated in Chapter 3, a truncated line out of *Inferno* V that describes Paolo and Francesca floating in the whirlwind of lust (che paion' si al vent': "who appeared so light on the wind") appears far back in Canto 110/777, and as late as Canto 80/499:533 Pound is still talking about descending into the depths of Hell in a line taken from *Inferno* V.86: "ma/cosi discesi per l'aer maligno" (but thus I descended through the malignant air).

It is more sensible to use Pound as the base rather than Dante for two reasons: 1) Dante's order is fixed and easily apprehended, but Pound's is not. When we approach the *Cantos* in the order in which they were written, we can view Pound's intellectual development historically. This is important because Pound's design was never as settled as Dante's; it was subject to sudden change, as in the dramatic developments around the *Pisan Cantos*. 2) Even though I have insisted that the various triads do not correspond exactly, this comparison allows us the added luxury of entertaining some notion of correspondence without insisting on it. At the start, the two writers may be quite divergent; at the end they may come closer together. Both reasons work toward a common end: we can see the *Cantos* as a constantly evolving entity, changing from the dynamic, turbulent mind of the youthful Pound, passing through a state of rigid dogmatism in the Middle Cantos, undergoing a personal purgative experience in the *Pisan Cantos*, and finally emerging in the Later Cantos as the mind of a chastened prophet lying beyond the fray. The rhythm of the *Cantos* is, in other words, genuinely the rhythm of the *Comedy*, but we still cannot approach the two works as if they showed a complete resemblance. The complex surface of the *Cantos* forbids it. Instead, we must comment on the general nature of each of the Dantesque canticles and then turn to the corresponding Poundian triads. This will help us to determine both the general similarities and the differences as a start. Then, using the *Cantos* as our base, we can look for Dantesque echoes and allusions in Pound's work, with an eye toward the changing nature of the modern poem. The *Comedy* will remain our intellectual constant; the *Cantos* will be our variable base.

*   *   *   *

The scheme of Dante's Hell is in part traditional and in part imaginatively unique. It is traditional to the extent that the region itself, with its various rivers and its location beneath the ground, was a part of the popular belief of the Middle Ages. Furthermore, such places as Cocytus, Acheron, Phlegethon, and the City of Dis were substantiated by Vergil's *Aeneid*. Even if Dante did take liberties in rearranging the locale into a descending cone, he can hardly be credited with conceiving its primary geographical features.

It is in the philosophical realm that we sense the Florentine's inventiveness. For example, the heat and brightness in a place called Hell (akin to modern German *hell*, "bright") are altered considerably, so that the region contains great variations. There is plenty of fire and brimstone, but the deepest place, which houses the lord of the realm, is a lake of ice. How did such changes occur? Undoubtedly through Dante's own imaginative probing, as well as through his awareness of the Neoplatonic cosmology, which tended to equate Hell or Non-Heaven with alienation, darkness, refractoriness, and chill rigidity. Certainly in avoiding the Miltonic pitfall of creating a fiery place with a fiery protagonist who threatens to dominate the work to the exclusion of the forces of good, Dante was able to give his opus a sense of philosophic balance, even if he did lose the Englishman's drama. Dante's Satan is foully repulsive, almost unmentionable; he is the culmination of those beastlike monsters that line the various circles of Hell like gargoyles on cathedral ramparts.

In fact, if we return to the Neoplatonic systems discussed in Chapter 3, we can see that Dante resembles them in his general conception of evil—what one might call his graphic or artistic conception of it—even if he is very different in his handling of detail. Dante's Hell corresponds to the Hyle or Dianoia section of the Neoplatonic world and body view: the senses, the emotions, matter, stuff. How physical the *Inferno* is! We can never forget the way that Pier della Vigna speaks with the rigidity of a man who is unable to bend; he is quite literally a tree, wooden and unyielding. Likewise Ugolino gnawing on the neck of Archbishop Ruggiero is every bit as cold, brittle, and unfeeling as the ice that imbeds the two. Gluttonous Ciacco lies like a piece of refuse discarded from a table. And certainly the tormented pain of Brunetto Latini, who runs forever on a burning desert in an aimless race with his fellow homosexuals, is a horrid example of flaming competition.

As we progress to the *Purgatorio*, we find that this second canticle is very much the place of Logos as it is in Neoplatonic systems. Logos is reason, paideuma, the Word, and all of the talk that goes on in the *Purgatorio* is toward education, toward straightening out Dante's previous crooked past. The *Paradiso* of Dante is similarly Neoplatonic: the place of Nous, Mind, and Spirit, the place where the body, freed from its limitations, partakes of the joy of free movement and harmony. Here Dante rejected the popular notion of Heaven as a pastoral location in the sky; instead, he took recourse to the traditional Neoplatonic imagery of light and systems of angelic hierarchy and planetary order.

From this brief analysis we may safely conclude that much of Dante's general vision follows the tradition of Plotinus, Porphyry, Proclus, Pseudo-Dionysius, Iamblichus, and Erigena, precisely where Pound always placed him. However, once we get down to details, we find that Dante's examination of evil is far more detailed than any we can find in almost any Neoplatonic philosopher. The typical Neoplatonic solution to the problem of evil (evil is a privation of the good without any substantial being) is clearly rejected by the Florentine in his embodiment of Satan and in the whole design of the

Inferno. To Dante evil was something very real. His insistence on
having Pier's body draped on his tree after Judgement Day seems to
pass beyond Catholic dogma to Dante's own very strong convictions
about the perpetuity of sin. Scotus Erigena would have found the idea
distasteful.

How, in fact, does a Neoplatonic talk about evil in the ethical
sphere? If we again use Erigena as our guide, we find that he barely
mentions the subject. Similarly if we go to St. Bernard of Clairvaux or
to Richard or Hugh of St. Victor, we simply do not find the kinds of
analysis of wrongdoing that appealed to Dante's empirical nature.
Dante had been severely wounded in life by calumny and vituperation. He demanded a system in return that could count hairs down to
the smallest number, one that would differentiate between barratry
and usury, and between simple and excessive wrath. As a result, he
had to consult that very different movement in philosophy: Aristotelianism.

It has long been a commonplace that Dante's *Inferno* owes a
great debt to Aristotle and to Scholastic comments upon him. The
Nicomachean Ethics probably did supply Dante with a great many of
his ideas—surely the notion, for example, of balancing one sin with
another, as in the Prodigality-Avarice confrontation in Canto VII.
Similarly the division of Hell into three units—Incontinence, Violence, and Fraud, in descending order—can be traced to Aristotelian
or Ciceronian sources. The details may be changed, for Dante was not
a slave to anyone's system. For example, one naturally does not find
the sin of Heresy in the Greek, since that aberration is possible only
with a dogmatic church, but it is a major trespass in medieval ethics.
What stamps Dante's Hell finally as his own is precisely his ability to
imagine. What medieval preacher would have put lust so high up in
his infernal scheme and counterfeiting so low? Dante's rather liberal
treatment of the Seven Deadly Sins (Envy is not even included in a
circle by itself) shows the way in which he again turned his back on
the popular mind, just as he excluded angels with harps of gold from
his Paradise.

When one has exhausted pagan sources like Aristotle and Vergil,
and when one has mentioned the precise, scientific nature of inquiry
patented by Scholastics like St. Thomas, and when one has ac-
counted for the cosmic sweep of the Neoplatonic vision, one must
finally say that Dante was in the last analysis a Catholic who insisted

upon the actuality of sin and the perpetuity of punishment. Dante wanted to convey the idea of Hell as an actuality; he wanted us to feel that if we were as cold-hearted as the murderer Fra Alberigo in Canto XXXIII, we would be unable to vent our passion; we would feel it constantly welling up inside our frozen skin. The mad cavortings of the devils and the grafters present City Hall life at its lowest level, just as Heresy is in a sense a lonely sin in which one is encased in a way that forbids human communication. But these psychological enactments of sin, dramatic as they are, are not meant to supersede the moral hierarchy that contains them. Even if the *Divine Comedy* is a vision that has appeared and vanished, Dante never lets us think for a moment that the world of the poem is itself a non-existent one, as the youthful Pound tended to imagine it in *Spirit of Romance*. The poetic manipulation of dogmatic belief is not meant in any sense to fancify that belief, although any non-Catholic reader is free to read as he chooses. This question of punishments and rewards in a life after death is possibly the biggest single difference between Dante's and Pound's minds and works. Pound does not so much reject the concept of a life after death as he is constantly unwilling to assert what he does not know.

Dante is thus blessed with a system that lends great order to his work, but one that is always threatening the life of his realistically conceived characters. Had he been as simplistic in his characterization as Guillaume de Lorris, he could easily have created a one-dimensional epic with Mr. and Mrs. Lust and Sir Gluttony instead of the vibrant Paolo and Francesca and the pathetic Ciacco. It would have been easy to knock over a series of cardboard villains and to set up a counterbalancing hierarchy of tinsel angels, but fortunately Dante's aesthetic sense forbade him this ease. Only in the gargoyle figures like Plutus, Cerberus, Minos, and Phlegyas do we get a sampling of the one-dimensionally bad, or in such lowly places as the eighth and ninth circles.

When it came time to people his Hell, Dante had the sense to use fully rounded men and women. He employs no dragons and dwarves and wizards from Arthurian romance; he uses Tristan in Canto V. The chthonic monster is included—can we ever forget Minos swinging his tail around or Medusa perched on the walls of the City of Dis?—but the human wrongdoer, the Farinata or the Cavalcante, dominates the action. These men are not unabashed villains totally devoid of dignity. Of course Farinata is overbearingly arrogant, but he is also noble and intelligent. Cavalcante is presented more as a loving father than as a satanic heretic. For all that Ulysses in Canto XXVI is stamped as an incitor to disaster, he still issues the call that was a manifesto for the finest humanists of the Renaissance:

> Men, consider your seed—
> you were not made to live like brutes
> but to pursue virtue and knowledge.   (118-120)

In short, Dante succeeds almost in spite of his system or in the tension that is created between himself as a moral judge and as an aesthetic creator. This tension is never more apparent than in the Limbo of Good Heathens in Canto IV. As we noted earlier, the word "honor" in one form or another resounds eight times here, like a dreary death-knell, as Vergil and he course over that ruined garden of Academe surveying the splendid minds of the past. The pride that Dante feels here is clearly shown in the proud repetitions of the word *vidi*, "I saw." Twelve times the verb rings through the canto, almost in triumphant contrast with the melancholy "honor." Like Caesar of old, Dante has regained the past, and even the magnificent people whom Christianity rejects he shores against the general ruin.

Pound was keenly aware of Dante's aesthetic dilemma when he said in Canto 116/797: "to excuse his hell/ and my paradiso." Dante, graced and cursed with a dogmatic structure that made things easy philosophically but difficult dramatically, was poet enough to rise out of these strictures and to create a comedy that was as human as it was divine. Ezra, on the other hand, never really could be sure that his work was assuming any kind of tangible form. Certainly it had "By no means an orderly Dantescan rising" (Canto 74/443:471).

In Chapter 3 we discussed the final solution that Pound seized upon for the construction of his *Cantos*. Being a Neoplatonic idealist by proclivity and a twentieth-century realist by birth, Pound could not accept the perpetuity of a place of punishment. He addressed himself entirely to this world, speaking often of the past and seldom of the future. He chose to speak of Dante's three regions as states of mind, and divided them into three areas: the ephemeral, the recurrent, and the permanent. Strictly speaking, Pound's Hell should have been simply a whirling place, a vortex, as it is in many of the Early

Cantos. His Underworld has a simple motto that is expressed in capitals in Canto 14: "THE PERSONNEL CHANGES."

Once Pound had chosen his system, he found himself in the same position as Dante: he was now a didactic poet who ran the risk of stifling his poetic characters. Pound's Hell Proper occurs in the so-called London Cantos, 14 and 15. Actually there is very little of London here; the place is, on the whole, quite indistinguishable, and the names of most of the inhabitants have rotted away. Usually one gets merely a series of slides and gestures:

> The slough of unamiable liars,
>   bog of stupidities,
> malevolent stupidities, and stupidities,
> the soil living pus, full of vermin,
> dead maggots begetting live maggots,
>   slum owners,
> usurers squeezing crab-lice, pandars to authority,
> pets-de-loup, sitting on piles of stone books,
> obscuring the texts with philology,   (Canto 14/63:67)

Here we see Pound's Hell working in conformity with his design, but it is not his Underworld at its most dramatic. Pound's Hell, almost by the rules that he had himself established, was bound to be a rather vague, undramatic place, somewhat like Dante's Judecca, where the primary movement is that of Satan grinding away with windmill mouths on the bodies of Brutus, Cassius, and Judas. In order to instruct effectively, Pound had to have coherent movement, and this becomes possible mainly in the central part of his poem, where we have tangible figures like Yong Tching, Thomas Jefferson, and John Adams to deal with, as well as such opposing forces as Alexander Hamilton, Nicholas Biddle, and William Paterson.

When we survey the Early Cantos, we find that rapid, whirling motion that we expect. Canto 1 is a general prelude to all of the *Cantos*, working much the way that *Inferno* I works for the *Comedy*. Here Pound, speaking through the persona of Odysseus, is dispatched by Circe to the brink of the western world, a world of "swartest night" and dark waves, in order to talk to the ghosts in Hades. This is a pre-Christian Underworld that reflects the general fate of mankind, without any particular judgements. Pound makes it sound more like an extension of this world than a place cut apart. In fact, Pound's Underworld is really just another name for the past, for history. Odysseus' journey is a collection of conversations, a string of thoughts, a chain of reveries existing in the timeless continuum of the poet's mind. We may hear of the "sunless dead" and a "joyless region," but we are not entering a Hell standardized by Dantesque judgements.

In fact, when we encounter Canto 2, we are soon aware of the lively vitality of the place. We experience a rapid, wild motion that becomes typical of the medium of expression of the Early Cantos. The yoking of Eleanor of Aquitaine with Helen of Troy indicates a blurring of historical identities, a movement toward archetypes. The fact that people and things change their shapes is made clear through the accounts of Ovidian characters like Tyro and the appearance of the god Bacchus among unbelievers. Proteus and the Oriental So-shu are there to reinforce the idea that nature is infinitely variable. From one point of view the Pentheus-Bacchus story is a minor tragedy; from another it is a tale of wonder. The important thing is to resist naming and judging shapes that we only barely apprehend. We must trust the fluid medium of Pound's narration to bear us on to certain islands of truth and clarity in the middle of the torrents of Nous.

In Canto 3 we are suddenly thrust into the twentieth century, sitting with Pound on the steps of the Dogana in Venice. Times are bad and the poet is broke, but around him is that permanent world of beauty toward which the *Cantos* are always striving. Pound thinks back to the world of the Cid, a world of romance and violence, which combines a kind of vigor with its danger. In Canto 4 we are plunged suddenly into "smoky light," into "dew-haze," where standards are again difficult to detect. We witness a series of violent acts: Itys is devoured by his father Tereus—but no, it is the troubadour Cabestan's heart being devoured by his beloved. Actaeon is being torn apart by his dogs—but no, it is Peire Vidal, who in wolf disguise is being attacked by dogs as he wooes his beloved Loba. We feel the naked force of myth breaking over us, inciting terror and awe and then . . . suddenly, almost as if the lighting had changed, we leave the dark woods of Actaeon's demise and enter a clearing where "the light rains . . . *e lo soleills plovil.*" The violent mythmaking of the Greeks and the Provençal troubadours yields to a sophisticated, domesticated vision of perpetual beauty: the pine trees set against the mountain at Takasago, the image of temple and mountain in a natural setting that recurs in various forms throughout the *Cantos*.

This image vanishes swiftly, like a tableau of Picasso, who is cited, incidentally, in Canto 2. Next we alternate between the spontaneous vigor of a marriage celebration, with echoes of Catullus and mentions of the South French city of Gourdon, and a few tranquil words from a Chinese-Japanese setting which state that "No wind is the king's wind," thereby asserting the common heritage of nature. We have a city, Ecbatan, and a beautiful woman, Danae, waiting for some benediction from the gods; there is talk about a communion between a Father Henri Jacques with the Sennin or gods on Rokku and there is a reprise of the Cabestan-Tereus myth. Thus Greece, Provence, and the Orient are constantly being brought into play together. Finally, almost as if the competing visions had reached a point of mystical clarity, we have a mention of a painting of the Madonna by Stefano da Verona, along with the citation of the name Guido Cavalcanti. We have moved, in fact, from wild, unchanneled violence through moments of more ordered vision, past a basic tenet (that nature belongs to us all), and have culminated with a Renaissance painting of a goddess, the Madonna. We have also lingered over what Pound considers quintessential things: the city, the temple, the mountain, the beautiful woman, the poet, the maker. Here in short we have the whole design of the *Cantos*. Yet this canto is itself merely one of seven leading up to the Malatesta group. It also stands in a spatial relation with the entire block of the thirty Early Cantos, and finally it is merely one panel out of the entire poem.

In Canto 5 we have the first important allusions to Dante. Although we might expect the first references to stem from the *Inferno*, we find that Pound mixes citations from the very start. After repeating the ideogram of bride-god-city and stressing that time "ticks and fades out," we move swiftly out of an earthly setting to a place removed from time:

> Measureless seas and stars,
> Iamblichus' light,
>   the souls ascending,
> Sparks like a partridge covey,
>   Like the "ciocco," brand struck in the game.
> "Et omniformis": Air, fire, the pale soft light.

This is clearly the world of Dante's *Paradiso*. In fact, the word "ciocco" is lifted out of XVIII.100 in the Heaven of Jupiter, where the general context reads:

Then as in the striking of burning brands
Arise innumerable sparks . . .

Poi, come nel percuoter d'i ciocchi arsi
surgono innumerabili faville . . .

This is a sudden mystic vision of light in which the exploding embers
are real spirits in the Dantesque passage, just as the ascending souls
are with Pound. The Latin translation of words of Porphyry, the
image from Dante, and the mention of Iamblichus form a Neoplatonic
ideogram that lifts us out of the ephemeral blur into a brief and lucid
glimpse of something eternal.

After that, however, the movement is again violent. We are
thrown down into a world of the troubadour-maker, where seduction
of women by men like Savairic Mauleon or Pieire de Maensac casts an
evil glow on their artistic creations. With the murder of Giovanni
Borgia we descend even lower to a Renaissance Italy that is cluttered
with "garbage" and "greasy stone," and where the cries of the
people are beastlike: "Dog-eye!" Here time is heavy upon us:
"Clock-tick pierces the vision." We are far from the timeless
stretches of the Empyrean. It is no wonder that the murder of Alessandro de'Medici should prompt the utterance of Francesca's curse
in *Inferno* V.107: *"Caina attende";* she is proclaiming that Caina,
one of the lowest regions of Dante's Hell, is waiting for her husband
and murderer, Gianciotto. This bitter outcry is followed in turn by a
quick mention of a "lake of ice," for that is how Caina is described in
Inferno XXXIII.

Canto 5 ends in a welter of hustle and bustle going apparently
nowhere: "Both sayings run in the wind." In the midst of this vortex
occurs another line from Dante: "Al poco giorno ed al gran cerchio
d'ombra" (With little daylight and with a great circle of shade). This is
the opening line of one of Dante's lyrics, a strange sestina written to
the so-called Rock Lady. It depicts the mysterious condition of a poet
wandering in a bewildering world of matter in which women have
hearts like stone, much like the world of Lucrezia Borgia and those
self-willed Renaissance women about whom Pound is writing here.
Dante's poem about Lady Matter—the term Madame "Hyle" (in
Greek script) occurs in Canto 30—is appropriate for establishing the
enigmatic world where a man like Mozarello has his life snuffed out
beneath a mule.

When we look at the canto as a whole, we can see that the movement is one of rapid change. The image of the brand struck in the game establishes a superior world of brilliant imagistic vision. The curse of Francesca acts as a judgement upon the evil deeds of the Borgias and the Medicis, while the mention of the lake of ice establishes the lowest possible moral pole. Between these two extremes falls the line of twilight identity from Dante's lyrics which helps to accentuate the shadowy background of most of Renaissance history, and which is the dominant medium of the Early Cantos. In every case, Dante acts like a moral barometer, measuring ethical valences. In the midst of Pound's perennially shifting texture, Dante helps us grope our way.

For example at the beginning of Canto 7 we have the now familiar Helen-Eleanor coupling, a snatch from Ovid, a mention of the welter of tourney life, and finally Dante's *ciocco* again. We would seem to have an ascending catalogue, but quickly we fall back from the flaming image of sparks shooting out of the brand to the very dull, dry scene that is in part lifted from the French prose of Flaubert. It is little more than a list of articles in a room. This is a pseudo-poetry of things, of mere stuff. Out of this "false marble" and these "darkish walls" comes a "great domed head, *con gli occhi onesti e tardi*" (with eyes honorable and slow-moving). This is an amalgamated line, stemming in part from a description of the Good Heathens in *Inferno* IV.112: *con occhi tardi e gravi* (with eyes slow and heavy), blended with a line from *Purgatorio* VI.63: *nel mover de li occhi onesta e tarda* (in the moving of those eyes honorable and slow), which describes the shade of Sordello. Both Sordello and the pagans are treated respectfully by Dante. We are not told who the Poundian phantom is who is "weaving an endless sentence," but the *Literary Essays* (p. 295) identify him as the writer Henry James. The Dante reference helps to make one thing clear: we should not denigrate the imposing figure. This "phantom with weighted motion" moving with heavy step, "drinking the tone of things," stands in contrast with the cheap ambience about him. The suggestions of Good Heathens and Sordello inform us that we must treat him as a kind of judging figure who is standing at odds with his age.

We continue to immerse ourselves in a tawdry civilization, an utterly material culture that Fritz (know Vanderpyl) describes aptly as one where you have a "Beer-bottle on the statue's pediment!"

Mentions of Eleanor and Helen recur, and the vision of a beautiful woman lifts us out of this desert into a flickering romantic shadowland with glimpses of "Lamplight at Buovilla" and "naked beauty." But this interlude does not last. It yields again to dry academic talk, to Ersatz fixtures, and to the "old room of the tawdry class." Suddenly Pound calls out a Dantesque line taken from *Paradiso* II.1, in which Dante addresses the reader whom he is about to draw behind him on his celestial flight:

> *O voi che siete in piccioletta barca*
>
> O you there in your little bark.

Pound is extremely fond of this line, using it frequently to encourage the reader to keep following him through difficult places, as in the last line of Canto 109: "You in the dinghey (piccioletta) astern there!"

Indeed the texture of Canto 7 continues to be murky. We encounter the romantic twilight world of Dido and Sicheus and then we return to a barren landscape with talk about hollow men and meaningless motion. Alessandro de'Medici is cited again briefly, this time as an "Eternal watcher of things,/ Of things, of men, of passions," almost as if his violent life is superior to the drone of modern existence. From there we jump to a mention of eyes floating in the air and talk about "stiff, still features." In the midst of this we have a very brief citation, "E biondo," which is probably meant to recall the much-quoted bravura description of Manfred in *Purgatorio* III.107: "biondo era e bello e di gentile aspetto" (Blond he was, and handsome—and with a genteel look). Like Manfred, Alessandro is a dashing aristocrat looming out of a dangerous world, but this world, for all of its violence, is superior to modern "pop" culture. Dantesque allusions, even truncated or amalgamated, serve as tabs which give us clues about the kinds of judgements we are to make in the highly variable, sometimes confusing fabric of Pound's poem.

The Malatesta Cantos, 8 to 11, loom as an island out of the vertiginous seas over which we readers have traveled. They are a place where a man can anchor, a place where there is something to hang on to. Pound is fond of attaching the character *chih*[3], 止 which resembles a hitching-post, to mark such points in the poem where he wants the reader to pause and consider. The character, which occurs at the end of Canto 52 among other places, means "stop, cease." In essence the Malatesta Cantos are to the Early Cantos what the New World and Adams Cantos are to the work as a whole: a buzzing center of purgatorial activity. Sigismundo builds his great Temple of Rimini out of veneration for his third wife, Isotta, and from a deep commitment to lasting beauty. He thus creates some stability out of the chaos around him. He patronizes the Neoplatonic philosopher Gemisthus Plethon, helping to introduce Greek studies to Italy and thus effecting that fusion of the classical with the medieval that produced the Renaissance. Similarly, his temple, though a Christian church, has many classical Greek elements in its architecture. Pound's own blending of Greco-Roman motifs with Provençal-Italian reflects the same process. Just as Sigismundo built his temple out of a hodgepodge of bricks and pillars and marble pieces, Pound constructs "the one Malatesta" out of scraps of documents and letters, for he believes that this is the way that beauty and truth are formed: they are hewn out of the ephemeral, using any and all materials at hand. Naturally in this section of the poem, where Pound is deeply committed to immediate facts, Dante has little to contribute.

If we take the Malatesta island and place it with Cantos 12 and 13, we have a clarification again of the over-all design of the *Cantos*. Sigismundo the Builder contrasts sharply with Baldy Bacon, the opportunistic entrepreneur, or with José Maria dos Santos, the glorified hog-dealer, or with the stiff Protestant bankers who listen to the off-color anecdote about the sodomitic merchant marine. Canto 12 is a Hell in one form or another, since it presents the cheap and the trite. Canto 13, on the other hand, is a brief vision of a kind of Paradise, and represents Pound's writing at its finest. His evocation of the figure of Kung (Confucius) walking by the dynastic temple and chatting in easy but memorable dialogue with his followers has the ring of eternal truth. The words and images are hewn as precisely as the finest Chinese print or the most trenchant lines of Sappho. This is something to enshrine. And although we are plunged directly from here into the center of Pound's Hell, we know from the start that there are certain values to which we are working. The Malatesta Cantos, Cantos 12 and 13, show the three kinds of poetic media that Pound uses throughout the poem. The cognitive functions that operate in them are those taken from Victorine epistemology that we established back in Chapter 3:

MALATESTA CANTOS	CANTO 12	CANTO 13
the recurrent	the ephemeral	the eternal
meditation (mind fixed upon objects for study)	cogitation (unfocused movement)	contemplation (mind at peace with object)
Purgatory	Hell	Paradise

Since the major portion of the Early Cantos proceeds in the style of Canto 12, we are safe in saying that on the whole these cantos do represent a form of the Inferno, but obviously, as the graph above illustrates, there is enormous variety in the texture.

Who but Dante should announce the opening of Hell Proper in Canto 14? "Io venni in luogo d'ogni luce muto" (I came to a place that was mute of all light). The words occur in *Inferno* V.28, where they describe Dante's entrance into the Circle of the Lustful. In Pound's pit we do not have the sexually maladjusted; we have:

> . . . the betrayers of language
> . . . . . . n and the press gang
> And those who had lied for hire;
> the perverts, the perverters of language,
>   the perverts, who have set money-lust
> Before the pleasures of the senses.

Pound's handling of detail is as precise as Dante's in such passages as:

> howling, as of a hen-yard in a printing-house,
>   the clatter of presses,
> the blowing of dry dust and stray paper,
> foetor, sweat, the stench of stale oranges,
> dung, last cess-pool of the universe.

One description is reminiscent of the popes who are stuck head-down in the baptistery-like font openings in *Inferno* XIX:

>   head down, screwed into the swill,
> his legs waving and pustular,

a clerical jock strap hanging back over the navel
his condom full of black beetles,
tattoo marks round the anus,
and a circle of lady golfers about him. (Canto 15/64:68)

In the main, though, Pound's two cantos seem much more general than the *Inferno*, perhaps because so many types are squeezed into so little space. Furthermore, there is a difference in intensity if not in method. Dante will employ burlesque, as with the counterfeiter Master Adamo and the treacherous Sinon of *Inferno* XXX, but usually he does not let his portrayals remain at this level. Even the hated Pope Nicholas III has a kind of dignity. Pound's denizens by contrast are "without dignity, without tragedy." Again and again Pound uses vulgar language: "the great scabrous arse-hole, sh-tting flies." Dante is capable of using a scatological line: *avea del cul fatto trombetta* (he had made a trumpet out of his ass, *Inf.* XXI.139), but he tempers his invective with humor. This brings up an interesting point of difference. Dante, with a dogmatic structure to back his poetic imagination, can afford to be liberal. Pound, constantly striving to create a sense of order, to hammer his points home, is forced to be much cruder and much more severe.

For all that Cantos 14 and 15 are frequently anthologized, they are not among the most memorable parts of the poem. Despite the drive for precision, the place is too busy, too peopled with unnamed people, to make the impression as intellectual as it is emotional. The few lines which owe something to Dante are not important: "In this *bolge* bores are gathered" (Canto 15/65:69) or "the beast with a hundred legs, USURIA" (64:68). One is far more likely to remember the vivid scene of Pound's escape with the help of Plotinus in Canto 16, with the naked running figures of Blake, Peire Cardinal, Sordello, and Il Fiorentino (The Florentine, Dante himself). Along with St. Augustine, who is inscrutably gazing toward the invisible, these men have all gotten out of Hell. After an acid-alkaline bath, Pound proceeds to examine the "mounts of cities," restoring the mountain and city images that help to form the central ideogram of the work.

Pound next passes into an idyllic grove with some classical nymphs, but this picture is shattered by an account of the needless ravages of World War I. Somehow this infernal section, with its colloquial French and dialect English, is more memorable than the preceding. Instead of hearing about such dry abstractions as "monopolists, obstructors of knowledge," we see the product of their work. We feel the hellish scene far more closely because we sympathize for its victims: T. E. Hulme, Wyndham Lewis, Gaudier-Brzeska, Hemingway, and others. The whole canto vibrates with drama and emotion. Here Pound seems to have learned something from Dante. Here, where he does not borrow directly from the Master, he shows that he is capable of creating a sympathetic portrait of the victim of corruption. He shows, in fact, some of that uncanny ability of the Florentine to evoke compassion for the lost. But the Pound of the 1920's and 1930's was in the main a self-assured, proud young artist who had little room for Pity, as he shows in Canto 30. Compassion was something he had to learn later.

After these explicit Hell sections, we return in Canto 20 to a beautiful, lush island that rises sharply out of the flux between the tawdry Hell of modern Manhattan in Canto 19 and the decadent splendor of Medicean Florence in Canto 21. It contains a variety of motifs, largely the paradisal ones concerning beautiful women, poetry, and love. Greek lyricism is transposed with Provençal. We encounter Pound, the budding editor and translator, journeying up to Freiburg to see the Provençal scholar Emil Levy, trying to decipher the puzzling word *noigandres*. The tranquility of this aesthetic toil is shattered by another scene of Renaissance lust relating to the incestuous acts of Parisina d'Este. This in turn leads to the formation of the idea that has long been lurking behind the Helen-Eleanor coupling about the nature of women:

Jungle:
Glaze green and red feathers, jungle,
Basis of renewal, renewals;
Rising over the soul, green virid, of the jungle,
Lozenge of the pavement, clear shapes,
Broken, disrupted, body eternal . . .
HO BIOS,
cosi Elena vedi   (91-92:95-96)

The last line consists of Dante's *Elena vedi* (See Helen!) of *Inferno* V.64 with a *così* or "thus" added to it. There is much disagreement about the line, for the *Annotated Index* translates it "thus Helen sees," and Pound's own gloss on it in a letter to his father calls it a "misquote of Dante" *(Letters,* p. 210). However the line is read, it refers to Dante's Hell, where Helen of Troy as temptress is named and judged. Pound is using her to affirm the potentially diabolical nature of woman, but the lines which follow change drastically:

> In the sunlight, gate cut by the shadow;
> And then the faceted air:
> Floating. Below, sea churning shingle.
> Floating, each on invisible raft,
> On the high current, invisible fluid,
> Borne over the plain, recumbent,
> The right arm cast back,
> > the right wrist for a pillow.

Here is the opposite picture of a woman as Venus recumbent after the fashion of Greek statuary, with a hint of Botticelli. This is woman in her counterbalancing role as angel-redeemer.

In the Early Cantos woman is usually portrayed as a potential source of destruction:

> Wein, Weib, TAN AOIDAN   (Wine, Woman, Song)
> Chiefest of these the second, the female
> Is an element, the female
> Is a chaos
> An octopus
> A biological process.   (Canto 29/144:149)

But Pound is more than well aware of her opposing nature. Dante's reference helps to establish the infernal nature here; but he also supplies some of Pound's redeeming women, especially Cunizza da Romano. Up to this point I have concentrated on Poundian verse allusions, ignoring such Dantesque characters as Cunizza, who appears in the Early Cantos, and Sordello and others. These people can best be treated later, when we have more of the breadth of Pound's poem to supply as a canvas for our comments.

Possibly the most important use of Dante's imagery occurs in Canto 23, where the famous phrase *selv' oscura* (dark wood) from *Inferno* I.2 falls on page 108:112. It follows a passage from the Greek of Stesichorus which describes the tenth labor of Hercules, who went in the boat of the Sun to seek out the cattle of Geryon. Pound connects this descent into darkness with the inquiries of scientists into the unknown: "Seeking doubtless the sex in bread-moulds." He then creates an important analogue: he links the Dark Ocean of Greek myth with the Dark Wood of Dante. Both are places of Matter, Evil, the Unknown, places of darkness where the light nevertheless can be found. All seekers such as Odysseus, Hercules, Dante the pilgrim, the scientist Curie, or Pound himself search for the light to illuminate these depths. They are all brethren in this respect. The Italian allusion brings Dante directly into focus with Homer and with the Aristotelians in Pound's pantheon. We thus have an ideogram with three members that can be related to the tripartite Neoplatonic system mentioned several times before:

Dark wood	Hyle, Dianoia	Hell
Seeker	Logos	Purgatory
Light Sought	Nous	Paradise

The lower members of the groupings are male; the upper member is female. However, woman is really capable of appearing anywhere on the chart, as we shall see when we study Cunizza. Madame Curie is implied with Monsieur Curie as a Seeker. Some of the primary dispensers of light are the goddesses and beautiful women of art who illuminate the later cantos. In fact, the variable role of woman in the *Cantos* is one of the factors that demonstrates the changeable quality of the poem.

Canto 23 falls itself into the tripartite rhythm that we have already observed many times. It opens with the light and fire of Intellect, with the names of two famous Neoplatonic philosophers, and with Latin words that suggest Porphyry:

> Et omniformis," Psellos, "omnis
> "Intellectus est." God's fire. Gemisto:
> "Never with this religion
> "Will you make men of the greeks.

It passes downward to a catalogue of objects that the scientist might study:

> How dissolve Irol in sugar . . . Houille blanche,
> Auto-chenille, destroy all bacteria in the kidney,
> Invention-d'entités-plus-ou-moins-abstraits-
> en-nombre-égal-aux-choses-à-expliquer . . .
>   La Science ne peut pas y consister. "J'ai
> Obtenu une brulure" M. Curie, or some other scientist

The canto then ends with darkness, destruction, and waves that have "No light reaching through them." Once again we have in capsule form a suggestion of the entire range of Pound's mind and the various sections of the poem.

In surveying the Early Cantos with an eye toward Dantesque allusions, we have seen the young Pound using the Italian master almost the way that a painter uses his colors: for emphasis and for dramatic effect. This brushstroke technique is nowhere more evident than at the end of Canto 24, when a picture of Ferrara passing into a phase of decadence is enlivened with a description of people who "read all day per diletto," after the fashion of Paolo and Francesca (*Inf*. V. 127). Pound's mind was saturated with Dante, and whenever he wanted to establish a moral climate, it was often the Italian upon whom he called. On reflection, some readers may find this simple transference of lines and motifs a bit facile. Certainly Dante enriches Pound, but the Dantesque lines sometimes stand out of the general surface of the *Cantos* a bit too boldly, as if calling an undue amount of attention to themselves. In turning to the Middle Cantos and beyond them to the *Pisan Cantos* we will find that the maturing Pound perfected his technique in a way that made his later Dantesque allusions a far more related, less imported part of the modern poem.

8

POUND'S TWO PURGATORIES: THE FICTIVE
AND THE REAL

When we place the Middle Cantos next to the *Purgatorio*, we see
perhaps the widest gap between the two epics. The *Purgatorio* shows
Dante in his most traditional Christian phase, struggling up the circles
around Mount Purgatory and working his way into the Earthly
Paradise. In a very general sense, this movement can also be traced in
Pound's Middle Cantos, for the reader struggles through the founding
of America and the Bank of Siena, reviews the massive achievement
of the Chinese dynasties, and finally returns to the New World of John
Adams, which is clearly cast in the perspective of an Earthly
Paradise. Both works deal with strivings for perfection: Dante's with
the perfection of his soul, Pound's with the perfection of states. The
greatest difference between them is that the Dante canticle is firmly
Christian, with the Seven Deadly Sins at its base, while the Poundian
section remains Neoplatonic and Confucian, in conformity with the
poem's earlier design.

Because Pound did not find the ritual activities of the *Purgatorio*
interesting enough to imitate, we do not find Dante in the Middle
Cantos with any of the frequency that occurs in other parts of Pound's
poem. One could say that the celebrated Usury Canto, 45, is primarily
Dantesque, but actually the Florentine is not mentioned directly, and
there are no clear-cut allusions. In fact, the Cavalcanti Canto, 36, is in
many ways more important for the entire section, as the reader who
glances back at the references in Chapter 5 will note. We must

remember that in the 1930's when Pound was working on this section of the poem, he was very deeply involved in his work on Guido. It is clear that the rational, heretical Cavalcanti at that time seemed more amenable to the milieu of Confucius and Adams than did his conservative Catholic friend. Recalling the guidelines established in Chapter 3, we must stress that Purgatory to Pound is quite simply a state of mind in which the reader-writer meditates upon the recurrent; it has nothing to do with Catholic rite.

Still, Dante is not by any means totally absent from the Middle Cantos. For example, Pound opens Canto 31 with his two American Paradise-carvers, Jefferson and Adams, establishing their dream of a society where the abundance of nature can exist for all. He ends it with a comparison of the England of 1814, a land that was filled with "paupers, who are about one fifth of the whole." The ineffectiveness of the French Revolution is contrasted with the achievement of the American. In Canto 32, Pound wishes to focus on the stature of Jefferson and Adams by placing them next to the second-rate minds of European nobility. We therefore have a roll-call: "Louis Sixteenth was a fool/ The King of Spain was a fool, the King of Naples a fool," and so on. At the end of this gallery of clowns we have the following:

> a guisa de leon
> The cannibals of Europe are eating one another again
> quando si posa.

The Italian lines describe the troubadour Sordello as he appears in *Purgatorio* VI.66, "like a lion/ when he is couched." Dante's description evokes the stern, moral qualities of that poet who wrote the rugged sirventes *Planher vuelh en Blacatz en aquest leugier so*, in which he invites the various titled heads of Europe to come and feast on his protector's heart in order to gain "heart" for themselves. Sordello gives Dante and Vergil a quick tour of the Vale of Princes, a niche where monarchs who were remiss in life are detained before they can ascend the mountain. Dante's section is filled with hope; Pound's is a mere rogue's gallery, using the Dante quotation to underscore the entire section with scorn.

Sordello is often used in Pound's work as the prototype of the emancipated poet who expresses morality with satiric wit and who is also capable of writing delicate verses of love. He occurs as early as Canto 2, where he is more the subject of a debate between Pound and

Browning about the uses of historical figures than a historical person-
nage in his own right. Sordello also appears in the important Canto 36
after the Cavalcanti translation. Here he is linked with Guido as a man
of vital action. We are told how "CHARLES the Mangy of Anjou"
granted him land because of his military and/or artistic merit, and we
have a line from one of his love poems: "Quan ben m'albir e mon ric
pensamen" (When I think well in my rich thoughts, ed. Boni, pp. 15
ff., st. 3). The Latin line "Sacrum, sacrum, inluminatio coitu" under-
lines the well-known erotic side of Sordello and connects him with
Cavalcanti, who firmly attached love to the senses. Dante saved the
troubadour from damnation, but Pound goes even further by putting
him on a philosophical plane with Cavalcanti and Scotus Erigena.

Pound does not try to cover up the scandalous side of Sordello's
past. He mentions the notorious elopement with Cunizza in Canto
6/22:26 and again in Canto 29/142:147:

> And sixth the Lady Cunizza
> That was first given Richard St Boniface
> And Sordello subtracted her from that husband
> And lay with her in Tarviso
> Till he was driven out of Tarviso
> And she left with a soldier named Bonius
> nimium amorata in eum
> And went from one place to another
> "The light of this star o'ercame me"

This elopement and estrangement would undoubtedly have caused
most of Dante's contemporaries to place the two in Hell. But Alighieri
saved them, putting Cunizza in his Third Heaven, the place inhabited
by those stained by earthly love. Similarly Pound scatters memories
of the two throughout his work. He uses a refrain from Sordello as late
as Canto 91/611:645: "pensar di lieis m'es ripaus" (the thought of her
is my repose).

The Sordello of the *Cantos* is a surrogate Pound, a morally
indignant poet who rails out against wicked politicians and who
undauntedly proclaims the beauty of love and sex. Sordello was
damned by the narrowminded for his indelicate behavior in Tarviso
(modern Treviso) just as Pound was attacked by the provincial bigots
of Crawfordsville, Indiana. By using him, Pound insists that the moral
fiber of a man—not the patina of romantic history—is what we must
search for. Similarly if Cunizza is branded by many as a high-class

whore, her boudoir life is not what interests Pound (who considers
that perfectly natural); what he grasps for is the fact that she freed her
serfs in the year 1265. She thus passes through a transfiguration in the
Cantos, from the high-living lady caught in the swirl of passing events
to a woman of significant action:

> In the house of the Cavalcanti
> > anno 1265:
> Free go they all as by full manumission
> All serfs of Eccelin my father da Romano
> Save those who were with Alberic at Castra San Zeno
> And let them go also
> The devils of hell in their body.   (Canto 29/142:147)

Another reference to Cunizza falls in the paradisal setting of Canto
92/620:653 with the words "fui chiamat'/ e qui refulgo" (I was called
[Cunizza], and here I glow). An allusion to her in Canto 74/443:465
shows that ultimately Pound linked her with the moon: "Io son la
luna' ". This association is developed further in Canto 76, where she
and other beautiful women form an ideogram of feminine beauty. Her
tripartite metamorphosis from slut to active giver to supreme lady of
beauty and mercy is thus completed. In Pound's poem Cunizza rises
above the welter of the common gossip and through a substantial act
of mercy joins the goddesses of love.

Another of Dante's *Purgatorio* characters whom Pound uses is
Arnaut Daniel, as in Canto 97/677:707: "Arnaut spoke his own language, 26th Purgatorio." His words are quoted in a modified form in
Canto 84/539:575: "quand vos venetz al som de l'escalina" (when
you come to the top of the stair) and in 83/529:564 with the single word
"*consiros*" (thoughtful). Pound was always impressed by the fact
that Dante let Arnaut speak in his own particular style. In fact, this
honor accorded to Arnaut may have eventually led to Pound's decision to include vast chunks of other languages in the *Cantos*, against
the express wish of most of his admirers. Pound abhorred provin-
cialism, and he saw Dante's espousal of Arnaut's language and culture as a form of internationalism long ahead of its time.

Pound uses Arnaut more in the Early Cantos than in any other
section. Two end-words from his sestina *Lo ferm voler qu'el cor
m'intra* are cited in Canto 6/21:25: "Ongla, oncle" (Nail, uncle). They
seem to do little more than to link the troubadour with a great woman,
the patroness Eleanor of Aquitaine. In Canto 20/89:93, Arnaut is

mentioned in a context with the indecipherable Provençal word *noigandres*, which inspired Pound's special trip to Freiburg to see Professor Levy. In Canto 29/145:150, Daniel's poetic ability seems to be set in contrast with the flow of the woman as a "biological process":

So Arnaut turned there
Above him the wave pattern cut in the stone.

Arnaut goes on to speak of the fear of life after death, but Hugh Kenner tells us in his *Pound Era* (p. 336) that the actual person was Eliot. In any case, Arnaut emerges as a sculptor of lines, a hewer of words. This is certainly the type of person who appears in Pound's Middle Cantos, but there is no place for Arnaut that cannot be more forcefully realized by other makers of beauty.

The same thing happens to another denizen of the Round of Lust, Guido Guinizelli. An adaptation of stanza 5 of his famous *Al cor gentil* opens Canto 51:

Shines
in the mind of heaven God
who made it
more than the sun
in our eye.

The lines are forcefully stated, but the source is not indicated. Guinizelli does not emerge as a person; he is merely blended in with the other Neoplatonics in the poem.

As Pound warms to his task in the Jefferson-New World Cantos, he links Dante to his basic thesis that history can best be understood in terms of economics. Canto 37 contains an account of the struggle of Martin Van Buren and Andrew Jackson against Nicholas Biddle and Alexander Hamilton, who were trying to perpetuate a privately controlled National Bank. Canto 37 passes from the victory of the two presidents to what Pound considered the catastrophe of modern life: the fact that privately owned banks control the abundance of nature that rightfully belongs to all. As the epigraph for Canto 38 we have a quotation from Dante:

> *il duol che sopra Senna*
> *Induce, falseggiando la moneta.*
>
> the grief above the Seine
> Brought on by falsifying the currency.

The source is stated: *Paradiso* XIX.118. At this place the Eagle of Jupiter is lashing out at the various rulers of Europe, much as Sordello did in the *Purgatorio*. The Eagle specifically accuses the French of falsifying the value of the coin, and this economic sin enters a roll-call consisting of nine tercets, three beginning with the initial letter L, followed by three beginning with U (V), and three with E. Put together, the anagram LUE may be the Italian word for "pestilence" or the Latin imperative "purify!" In either case, Dante's talking bird sounds exactly like Uncle Ez, and the deliberate accusation in economic terms strengthens Pound's notion that Dante shared his monetary interests. The mere dropping of the word "Senna" in Canto 97/671:702 shows Pound's insistence on this belief.

The induction of Alighieri into the Pound camp is complete with the extensive use of the hellish monster Geryon in Cantos 49 and 51. Dante introduces Geryon in *Inferno* XVI as a device for getting himself and Vergil from the Seventh Circle of the Violent to the Eighth Circle, the first of the last two rounds devoted to Fraud. Geryon is a fearsome beast:

> His face was the face of the just—
> benign in its look in the flesh exposed
> but the rest—a snakey trunk.
> Two paws he had, hairy up to the armpits,
> and back and breast and both his flanks
> all painted over with knots and little wheels.
> Tartar or Turk never fashioned stuff
> more gaudy in groundwork or embroidery,
> nor Arachne in webs spun upon her loom.   (XVII.10 ff.)

Doubtlessly Pound saw a likeness between Geryon's painted skin and the gaudy pouches of the usurers, who sit crouched on the rim of the Seventh Circle. Fraud and Usury were thus inextricably linked in his mind, just as he no doubt interpreted the knots on Geryon's skin as the knots of Solomon, traditional symbols of usury. At any rate,

Dante's feverish flight on the monster's back made a great impression on the modern poet. When it came time to construct his own epic, Pound adapted the monster in a very direct way. For example, the lovely paradisal flow of Canto 49 is shattered by these lines:

> State by creating riches shd. thereby get into debt?
> This is infamy; this is Geryon.

The adaptation is more extended in Canto 51 when, after the much-quoted lines on Usury, we have a brief flight that mimics Dante's more protracted one:

> circling in eddying air; in a hurry;
> the 12: close eyed in the oily wind
> these were the regents; and a sour song from the folds
> of his belly
> sang Geryone; I am the help of the aged;
> I pay men to talk peace;
> Mistress of many tongues; merchant of chalcedony
> I am Geryon twin with usura.

It seems extraordinary for a twentieth-century poet to use a medieval gargoyle figure in such an extended way. One can hardly imagine Yeats or Eliot doing the same. But Pound's fixation on money crimes leads him to adopt the patently pedagogical manner of the medieval moralist, as we can see in Cantos 88/583:619 and 97/675:705. Only in Canto 111/783 does the monster figure seem to be employed in a way that goes beyond the merely didactic:

> Gold* mermaid up from black water—
> Night against sea-cliffs
> the low reef of coral—
> And the sand grey against undertow
> as Geryon—lured there—but in splendour,
> Veritas, by antithesis, from the sea depth
> *come burchiello in su la riva*
> *Later editions have "Cold"

Pound gazing down into the waters sees an image of golden beauty swimming up to him, then sees it transformed as the mermaid becomes a beast. He sees, in fact, the antithesis operating in the same field with the ideal (veritas), almost as mimicry; for what is a gargoyle but a fallen bird of beauty?

When we turn to the *Comedy,* we see that Dante was enormously surrealistic in his own approach. In fact, he devoted more than a canto to the simulated flight and to minute descriptions like the one that Pound modifies in the last line above: "like a little boat upon the bank." In *Inferno* XVII.19, Geryon is likened to a boat, half perched on the shore and half jutting into the water. Dante goes on to compare the beast to a beaver, with his tail wiggling out in the water before he leaps on some prey. The whole picture is simultaneously imaginative and precise. The ride itself is like a fantastic swan-ride into an ethereal depth, but in this case the depths are down rather than up. Dante employed fantasy for a hard, practical end. Here Pound shows a kinship with the master, for he suggests that as one looks into the depths of the mind, fixating upon beauty, he may see the form of its opposite; both exist; neither should be denied. Pound is very much like Scotus Erigena, who would not banish the evil from active participation in the future life, but saw them trailing along in some inexplicably recalcitrant way in the great dance of the beyond.

With Canto 52, we enter the Chinese Cantos. Here on page 259:269, at what may have once been envisioned as the middle-point of the poem, Pound wrote two important lines:

> Life and death are now equal
>   Strife is between light and darkness.

From this point on in the *Cantos* there is a significant increase in the light symbolism, and a suppression of the more obviously grotesque. Undoubtedly Dante's own handling of light inspired much of Pound's, for the dark horror of the *Inferno* lingers in every reader's mind, just as the beautiful description of the dawn in *Purgatorio* I and the fiery formations of planetary lights in the *Paradiso* remain unforgettable. But once again Pound does not adopt a formal handling of the imagery; he shifts his field constantly.

Dante's influence is especially slight in the Chinese and Adams Cantos. Later in Canto 89/604:638 we hear that President Andrew

Jackson admired "his (Dante's) in'elect," but no attempt is made to relate his presidential predecessors directly to the Italian. Nevertheless, a series of quotations from Canto 69/407:430 will attest to Dante's continuing presence in Pound's mind. Three citations follow hard after a list of people who have "gone piss-rotten for Hamilton" and for the aristocratically controlled, monopolistic National Bank. We have the words "natural burella," meaning "natural hole," cited from *Inferno* XXXIV.98, the bottom of Dante's world, to show how low we have sunk. Next we have:

> squad of the pink-haired snot
> traitors blacker than Arnold
>   blacker than Bancroft
> *per l'argine sinistra dienno volta.*

The last line, adapted from *Inferno* XXI.136, describes the pompous movement of the demons guarding the barrators in the Fifth Bolgia of the Eighth Circle: "they turned left by the dyke." The guardians of the barrators with their serio-comic gestures are, Pound thinks, like the followers of Hamilton. The portrait ends:

> behind the mask Mr Schuyler (Filippo)
> these the betrayers, these the sifilides
> advance guard of hell's oiliness
> in their progeny no repentence (*sic*)
> *quindi Cocito, Cassio membruto*

The last line is a composite drawn from *Inferno* XXXIV.52 and 67: "Thus here is Cocytus," the lake of ice; and here is "Cassius the big-membered," one of the three figures being devoured in the triple mouths of Satan. The "Filippo" connects the wrathful Argenti of *Inferno* VIII with Schuyler. Although America is the Earthly Paradise for Pound and the general hum of the canto is one of purgatorial energy, there are always hellions in the garden. Dante, as he did so often in the Early Cantos, helps to pin them down.

At the close of the Adams Cantos, Pound as poet and propagandist sounded very certain that he was helping to create a new Earthly Paradise in Italy. Dante enters a garden of perfection after he climbs the rugged hill, and similarly in the two long-missing but now retrieved cantos after 71 Pound is said to have discussed Mussolini's Italy in terms of praise. But unfortunately for Ezra, history shattered his dreams, and his Utopia receded as far from actualization as Dante's pastoral garden was removed from reality. But if Pound did not find social perfection realized, he did discover his own humanity, and this new-found mercy or pity—so violently rejected in Canto 30—is what redeems the Later Cantos. Since the *Pisan Cantos* are a bridge to the *Rock-Drill* and *Thrones Cantos*, they can be discussed either here or as part of the final section. I choose to treat them here, because of their truly purgatorial nature. This is the place where Pound, like Alighieri, joins those "who have passed over Lethe" (Canto 74/449:477), the river of forgetfulness in *Purgatorio* XXVIII, where Dante had to acknowledge his sins and then obliterate them as he passed on to higher things. At this point, the *Cantos* become more than a series of epic narrations; they become a personal threnody in a tragic rhythm: the movement of confession, catharsis, and satisfaction, as the poet finally drops his many masks and confronts us with his self.

*   .   *   *   .   *

With the writing of the *Pisan Cantos*, Pound's tone changes considerably. Gone is the defiant, assured, self-confident voice that one hears throughout the Adams and Chinese Cantos. Instead, one catches the plaintive, searching cadences of a man sitting in the midst of ruins and looking back over his life, trying to find what went wrong inside himself and outside, and wondering what can be salvaged from the debacle. At this point in the writing of the poem, Pound finds a new proximity to his Italian predecessor, and references to Dante increase considerably.

The way in which Pound uses Dante in the *Pisan Cantos* differs sharply from the brushstroke technique of the Early Cantos. For example, the line "Tre donne intorno alla mia mente" (Three ladies around my mind), which occurs in Canto 78/483:514, provides an immediate comment on the passage which precedes it. Pound's line is adapted from the opening of one of Dante's most famous lyric poems: *Tre donne intorno al cor mi son venute* (Three ladies have come around my heart). In the Italian poem Dante is haunted by a vision of three allegorical women, who stand for Justice, Generosity, and Temperance, and who come begging in weeds because of the generally debased nature of contemporary life. They besiege Dante's heart (Pound's mind), and cause him to suffer a high-pitched melancholy in his exile, which may be actual, spiritual, or both. Pound finds himself in Dante's same alienated situation, but instead of seeing three allegorical women, he sees three actual women:

Cassandra your eyes are like tigers' . . .
eyes of Doña Juana la loca,   (the mad)
Cunizza's shade al triedro . . .   (at the corner)

They do not lecture to him; they simply assure him of the endurance of beauty in his time of need. Around him are the American "sargeants" and the memories of the boredom of caged animals in zoos; but the vision of the women and the natural setting finally rescue him:

Tre donne intorno alla mia mente
but as of conversation to follow,
boredom of that roman on Olivia's stairs . . .
and as for the solidity of the white oxen in all this
    perhaps only Dr Williams (Bill Carlos)
        will understand its importance,
its benediction. He wd/ have put in the cart.

Here is no mere playing with Dantesque themes. Here is a direct transferral of Dante's imagery and state of mind into Pound's similar situation.

The real contribution of Dante to the *Pisan Cantos* comes from Pound's skillful adaptation of *Commedia* characters, especially those from the *Inferno*. Pound, in Hell himself, suddenly sees Dante's creations in a far more personal way. For example, the following echo of Dante in Canto 74/435:462 does more than merely transfer a sharp image:

for this stone giveth sleep
      staria senza più scosse
and eucalyptus that is for memory
under the olives, by cypress, mare Tirreno.

The Italian line means "would stand without more shakings." It is taken from *Inferno* XXVII.63, where Guido da Montefeltro, encased in a flame that wavers back and forth whenever he exerts himself, addresses the pilgrim Dante, whom he mistakes for another member of the dead. I shall translate the opening lines, which Eliot used as the epigraph for "The Love Song of J. Alfred Prufrock":

> "If I believed that my reply would ever
> fall on the ears of one who'd return to Earth,
> this flame would stand without any further sways (*scosse*);
> but since no living man once yet—
> if I hear right—reissued from these depths,
> without any fear of infamy I'll speak."

The words are crafty, bitter, but somewhat resigned to a state of damnation. They embrace the listener as a fellow in Hell, finding a certain comfort in the companionship. It was Eliot's way of putting both Prufrock and his reader in the same cursed position. Pound, in that position literally, employs the line in a sympathetic way, for Guido's pain is his pain. Unlike Guido, however, he has nature to fall back on: the healing caress of the eucalyptus and cypress (with mad Ophelia's language hovering over the images), the natural scenery of the Tyrrhenian Sea. Dante's line supplies us with a sense of hellish torture, but this pain is brought into balance or suspension by the magic elements around it. The line is not just a borrowing. It conveys the agony itself.

Somewhat similar is the mention of Ugolino in Canto 74/436:463, still in the same passage. To supply some mental balm, Pound reviews some scenes of natural beauty:

> Past Malmaison in field by the river the tables
>   Sirdar, Armenonville
> Or at Ventadour the keys of the chateau;
>   rain, Ussel,
> To the left of la bella Torre   the tower of Ugolino
> in the tower to the left of the tower
>   chewed his son's head
> and the only people who did anything of any interest were
>   H., M. and
>   Frobenius der Geheimrat

The cityscape of Pisa provides a constant background for the *Pisan Cantos*. As visions of remembered French châteaux and towns yield to the scene at hand, Pound's eye falls on the Leaning Tower and then the other tower in which Ugolino of *Inferno* XXXIII recounts his imprisonment and his subsequent death by starvation. The fact that he devoured any of his sons, who were imprisoned with him, is a mere assumption on Pound's part, for the Italian is ambiguous: *Poscia, più che'l dolor, pote 'l digiuno,* "afterwards more than grief hunger did its work."

Dante's handling of the figure is quite complex, for he conveys the man's aristocratic power brought to a low pathetic condition. Ugolino suggests as much the towering noble as the brute cannibal. Pound draws upon these overtones, applying them to his own condition. The Gothic, shadowy tower with its suggestions of unjust murder and unjust revenge relate directly to Pound's immediate confinement, for Pound's situation at the time of the writing was every bit as precarious as Ugolino's. Yet besides suggesting violence and romantic horror, Ugolino functions as a semi-heroic figure with whom Pound can align. Outcasts like Ugolino are far superior in Pound's own mind to the boring, do-nothing world which is catalogued in the lines that follow. Ugolino is used in a twofold way: as a tragic figure brought low with whom Pound can identify and also as a romantic figure trapped by circumstances beyond his control, who lends Pound courage. In any case this is no simple adoption.

Pound uses allusions to two other tragic figures from the *Inferno* back-to-back in Canto 79/487:519:

> Bless my buttons, a staff car/
> si come avesse l'inferno in gran dispitto
> Capanaeus
> with 6 on 3, swallow-tails

Although a fixed interpretation of this passage is difficult to establish, the references are apparent. Capaneus is a great rebellious figure, one of the legendary Seven Against Thebes. He is encountered in *Inferno* XIV.43 ff., where he is bound against the ground in a rain of fire, and he rails out violently against God as a blasphemer. He serves as little more than an exemplum of pride: "O Capaneus, as far as your pride was not checked, thus far are you punished" (63 f.). Vergil further remarks that *"par ch'elli abbia/ Dio in disdegno"* (it seems that he holds God in disdain). These words are partially felt in Pound's Italian, which reads "as if he held Hell in great disdain," but actually this line derives directly from *Inferno* X.36, in a passage that describes the lordly Farinata, whom we mentioned in Chapter 4. The pertinent lines from that passage are:

> Already I had fixed my face upon him
> while he was raising brow and breast,
> as if he held all Hell in great disdain.   (34-36)

Dante's portrait never for a moment lets us condemn Farinata in the way that we measure Capaneus. Farinata is aristocratic in the finest sense, even if he is arrogant and apparently a heretic.

Returning to the passage from Canto 79, we find that the automobile of an American officer interrupts Pound's meditative study of birds sitting in complex patterns on telephone wires. Pound seems at first to direct Dante's Capaneus allusion to one of the occupants of the car, who looks out of place in his official splendor in the squalor of the concentration camp, and who perhaps views it with the disdain of a Farinata. But in the rapid flux of the lines, one begins to feel that the officer's arrogance is transferred to the poet himself, and that Ezra rises out of the meaningless interruption of pompous authority and asserts his proud though pathetic right to indulge in his meditation of the swallowtails. Pound becomes Farinata, becomes Capaneus. He sees himself as a Dantesque character in the American Army's Hell, and he refuses to grovel there. If Dante endowed Farinata with an incontestable tragic splendor, Pound restores to the dead Ghibelline even more of the epic glow by imbibing the man's hybris. For Pound is fully aware of the double nature of pride. As he insists in Canto 77/473:503, Farinata was among those

> who resisted at Arbia when the fools wd/ have burnt down
> Florence "in gran dispitto" "men used to obeying orders"

Similarly in Canto 92/618:651 Pound connects Farinata with heroic deeds:

> And honour?
>   Fitzgerald: "I was."

When he freed a man
  who had not been at the Post Office . . .
accused of not taking cover during bombardment.
                 "Gran dispitto."

Actually Pound's assessment of Farinata does not stem from Dante alone, but also from the realm of art, as is shown clearly in Canto 78/480:512:

So he said, looking at the signed columns in San Zeno
"how the hell can we get any architecture
              when we order our columns by the gross?"
red marble with a stone loop cast round it, four shafts,
and Farinata, kneeling in the cortile,
        built like Ubaldo, that's race,
Can Grande's grin like Tommy Cochran's

Through the painting Pound raises Farinata to a level with Can Grande della Scala, Dante's great patron. Doubtlessly the ordeal at Pisa had caused Pound to readjust certain standards. Although Pound's most celebrated passages of the *Pisan Cantos* concern the relinquishing of pride, there is no doubt that he had to assert his own toughness to survive the nightmare of Pisa, and Dante's denizens of Hell were there to assist him.

Another *Inferno* figure who occurs here is Bertran de Born, the renowned troubadour who had fascinated the lyrical Pound in such adaptations as "Near Périgord" and "Sestina: Altaforte." Dante dealt harshly with Bertran, putting him among the Sowers of Discord in *Inferno* XXVIII.118 ff., where he appears holding his head like a lantern in his hand. Dante had pronounced his judgement upon Bertran because of a series of blistering poems which Bertran launched against a variety of people, including Richard the Lion-Hearted and King Philip Augustus of France. Pound never accepted the severity of this sentence and, in fact, in "Near Périgord" he probed Bertran's state of mind, trying to find a strategic justification for the man's perennial dissatisfaction. Pound asked the question: how would you like to live in a castle that you had to share with one brother, and possibly two—with your back against the wall?

The historical facts about Bertran's dilemma are contained in his poem *Un sirventes on motz no falh* (ed. Appel, 1932, pp. 31 ff.: I'll write a satire where not a word fails). It is true that Bertran is often passionate to the point of being bloodthirsty, as Dante had suggested. His *Be.m platz lo gais temps de pascor* (ed. Appel, pp. 92 ff.: How I like the gay time of spring) is a call to battle, not a spring song, as the opening line might indicate. In his final lines, he shows his sense of the economic background for war when he proclaims:

> Barons, put up as pawns
> Those cities and castles and villas
> Before you bring each other war!

> *Baro, metetz en gatge*
> *Chastels e vilas e ciutatz*
> *Enanz qu'usquecs no.us guerreiatz!*

Pound interpreted those words as meaning: let the usurers pay! They tickle his heart, as he shows by quoting them partially in Cantos 85/548:584 and 105/749:774. To Pound, Bertran is another powerful satirist cut after the model of Sordello and Peire Cardenal. From his point of view, Dante was exercising an incomplete judgement by putting Bertran so deep in his Hell.

   But the Bertran railing out against his time and insisting that combat must be put on a cash basis is not the Bertran who comes through most movingly in the *Pisan Cantos*. As Pound was well aware from his youthful translation, Bertran was a sensitive poet when he cared to be. He wrote a *planh* or lament on the death of Henry, the young son of Henry II of England, that ranks as one of the finest threnodies in the annals of world literature. The opening line, taken from the 1932 edition of Carl Appel (pp. 98 f.) reads: *Si tuit li dol e.lh plor e.lh marrimen:* "If all the sorrow, the tears, the suffering." Pound cites part of this line in memory-emended form in Canto 80/516:550, and again in 84/537:572. The first citation is a moving lament over the dead of the past, including places and things that he fears that he will never again see:

> That would have been Salisbury plain, and I have not thought of
> the Lady Anne for this twelve years
> Nor of Le Portel
> How tiny the panelled room where they stabbed him
> In her lap, almost, La Stuarda
> Si tuit li dolh ehl planh el marrimen
> for the leopards and broom plants.

Bertran's words add a majestic solemnity to Pound's own dirge over time gone by, which continues magnificently:

> Tudor indeed is gone and every rose,
> Blood-red, blanch-white that in the sunset glows
> Cries: "Blood, Blood, Blood!" against the gothic stone
> Of England, as the Howard or Boleyn knows.

Ezra and Bertran were both hell-raisers; but they were kindred too in their love of beauty and tradition. Almost as if Bertran were standing behind him, guiding him, Pound rediscovers his love for that land that he so often vilified, a land that Bertran knew probably only through the children of Eleanor:

> and the Serpentine will look just the same
> and the gulls be as neat on the pond
> and the sunken garden unchanged
> and God knows what else is left of our London
>   my London, your London

Bertran and Ezra, both so quick to judge and so slow to forgive, become one. Dante is left somewhere in the background.

In the main, the *Pisan Cantos* show Pound's ability to use Dante as a springboard for developing his own personae and ideas. But in one respect the two are very close: the attitude toward Fortune. Most medieval philosophers and theologians seemed to regard the concept, if at all, with contempt. Following Boethius, who created the allegorical figure only to dismiss her, they could find no room for Lady Luck in a system where Providence ruled worldly goods. However, the mature Dante saw things in a radically different light. Having suffered exile, humiliation, and want, he could not believe that Justice prevailed on Earth. Therefore in *Inferno* VII.70 he provided one of the most authoritative presentations of Fortune's operation in world literature. Dante the pilgrim asks Vergil about the workings of the goddess, and the Roman replies as follows (with Italian glosses in places where Pound took borrowings):

> . . . "Foolish creatures!
> How great is the ignorance that offends you!
> Now I want you to imbibe my words of wit.

He Who transcends all your mortal knowing
fashioned the heavens and gave them a power
that conducts in equal proportions the light
so that it shines from every part to every part.
In the same way for all the worldly splendors (*splendor mondani*)
He ordained a general minister and guide
who would change from time to time (*che permutasse a tempo*)
the paltry goods from tribe to tribe, blood to blood,
beyond any prevention by your human sense,
so that now one people rules, another lapses,
following the judgement that she gives,
which is as hidden as a snake in the grass.
Your knowledge can offer no contest against her,
for she foresees, she judges, she executes
her realm as do the other gods their own.
Her changes will admit no kind of truce;
necessity it is that makes her swift;
so quickly does one come to effect his turn.
She it is who's put up on the cross
even by those who ought to give her praise,
giving her blame (*biasmo*) with a wrong and wicked tongue.
But she is blessed (*beata*) and does not hear.
With the other primal creatures, happily
she spins her sphere and, blesséd, she enjoys (*beata si gode*).

This is an extraordinary piece of philosophical poetry, for it establishes Fortuna as the planetary Intelligence for Mother Earth. Every sphere or planet has its ruling power, and Earth, which seems to have none, is thus given Dame Luck, whose essential nature is that of change. Dante's account of Fortuna goes beyond mere acceptance to the point of deification.

Pound, perhaps not so strangely, came to esteem this passage relatively late. In *Spirit* (p. 111), he seemed to honor Fortune as another pagan deity who survived the Christian era, but in his Early Cantos he did not employ her. Only after the catastrophic downfall of Mussolini was he fully prepared to acknowledge the bitter wisdom of Dante's words. The Fortune motifs begin as late as Canto 76/456:484 with words from Charles d'Orléans: "Tout dit que pas ne dure la fortune" (Everything says that fortune does not last). The line is elaborated upon in Canto 86/566:602 with the statement: "but man is under Fortuna," followed by the Chinese character which Pound marks *chên* and the Italian words *La donna che volgo*. These last words are taken from the opening line of one of Cavalcanti's poems printed in *Tre Canzoni of Guido Cavalcanti: Io sono la donna che volgo* (I am the lady who turns). In Canto 96/656:687 we have a repetition of the Chinese ideogram *chen*⁴ with the words "all under the Moon is under Fortuna" above it and "e che permutasse" below. Apparently Pound extracted the moon reference from Dante, for elsewhere, as in Canto 91/613:647 he correctly allies the Chinese character with "thunder." *Chen*⁴ 震 is 315 in the *Mathews Chinese-English Dictionary*, and means "to shake, excite, terrify." King Lear, an old man who braved the elements like Dante and Pound and went on to achieve wisdom, is mentioned just above it, and the magician Merlin below.

Two other Fortune citations occur in Canto 97; first on pages 676:706, we have:

> All neath the moon, under Fortuna,
>   splendor' mondan',
> beata gode, hidden as eel in sedge,
>   all neath the moon, under Fortuna

and on 677:708:

> Earth under Fortuna,
>   each sphere hath its Lord,
> with ever-shifting change, sempre biasmata,
>   gode.

Even in the fragment of Canto 112/785 we have an echo of the motif, with a crude drawing presenting the winnow of "fate's tray" and a half-moon with the word "luna" beside it.

In the *Pisan Cantos* we see for the first time a true assimilation of Dante in Pound's work. In the Early and Middle Cantos, Pound toyed with Dante's images and themes without really making them a part of himself. But in the *Pisan Cantos* when he was forced to reassess his life and re-estimate the value of everything he held dear, Dante's images and characters suddenly emerged with a new and vital expressiveness. Dante's citizens of Hell merged with Pound himself, lending him sustenance; they were no longer mere personae waiting for adaptation. Feelings of guilt, suffering, and finally compassion suddenly showed in Pound's writing in a way that made clear their absence in the earlier work. We may say that the *Pisan Cantos,* in fact, constitute a true purgation for the work, as meaningfully as does the ritual act of Dante atop Mount Purgatory. In a golden flow of words, the *Cantos* transform themselves from an intellectual exercise into a genuine expression of the self. In Pisa, at a time of grave danger, in the shadow of death itself, Dante loomed as master and friend to the man in the gorilla cage.

9

TWO HEAVENS OF LIGHT AND LOVE:
THE VISIONS OF OLD AGE

It takes a great deal of nerve for anyone to write a *Paradiso*, and the two authors under scrutiny were well aware of the hybris involved. Dante, of course, had an easier task, since there was a prevailing notion of a judgement in a life after death in the society around him. Pound, living at a time when many doubted an afterlife, had to seriously question any possibility of a state of perfection either inside or outside of the earthly existence. But if Dante stood on surer theological ground, the aesthetic problems raised by his celestial flight were great. The lack of dynamic characters in the outer stretches of the journey definitely impedes a full appreciation of the work for many readers. Even in the lower spheres, many people do not share Pound's interest in Justinian or Folquet of Marseille as Dante presents them.

However, Dante never let aesthetic considerations stand in the way of his philosophic intentions. Clearly to him Heaven was a place where the ego of personal identity had to yield to the all-embracing abstract identity of Nous. To sprinkle his *Paradiso* with vivacious characters would amount to undermining the whole notion of tranquility of a mind turning toward the contemplative vision that closes the work. In the rabble of wild cogitation that forms the underlying rhythm of the *Inferno*, the dynamics of the personality were essential. That was the world of ego and emotion. In the meditative concentration of the *Purgatorio*, a man's self could express itself with some of the old passion that was gradually being restrained by the bit, especially in the form of flashbacks. But in Paradise proper, the realm of contemplation, where we move toward that still center of the rose that is the culminating vision of the work, we must play down the dissonant sounds of the emotions and float on the harmony of image and pure form. From Canto XXX onward, as symbols and visual figures replace discursive language, the poem moves to a close that is hauntingly dreamlike. Pound always appreciated the visionary qualities here; he never saw the journey as a historically documented event. He was sure that Dante had never gotten any nearer to Venus and Mars than he had. He always saw the entire trip as the presentation of three vivid states of mind, with the emphasis on the searching rather than on the finding. Pound further felt that Dante's language was its most precise and daring at this point in the poem, exactly when the danger of vague abstraction was greatest.

Fully aware of all of the risks involved, Pound decided to write a poem that touches on the three Dantesque spheres. I will not say that the Later Cantos form an exact parallel with Dante's *Paradiso*, but I will frankly admit that there is a strong heavenly cast to much of the rhetoric. There are many clues in the Later Cantos that Pound is attempting to reach stratospheric heights. For example, the lines "to enter the presence at sunrise/ up out of hell, from the labyrinth" (Canto 93/632:664) indicate a passing upward from the contorted context of the Early Cantos. The beautiful dawn scene of *Purgatorio* I.115-17, with the gentle rustle of the sea, is recalled in Canto 92/620:652: "And from afar/ il tremolar della marina." Similarly the line "Alighieri, a rag over his eyes" in Canto 100/718:746 seems to be a reaction to the blinding light (characters *pai jih,* 白日 "white sun") which precedes it; this is the blinding light of the Empyrean. Furthermore Pound himself has frequently spoken in special terms of this last third of the work, as in a letter to George Santayana written on December 8, 1939: "I have also got to the end of a job or part of a job (money in history) and for personal ends have got to tackle philosophy or my 'paradise' " *(Letters,* p. 331).

We must now distinguish between two kinds of presentations of a Heaven. Dante treated his Paradise as an ethereal, abstract place, having nothing to do with the traditional Elysian Fields or with a Utopian city. Pound will not settle for this cosmological setting. From the Early Cantos onward, we see the holy city emerging as a central

part of the basic ideogram of the work. Pound's Paradise is at its base
a terrestrial one, and far more urban than pastoral. He absolutely
refuses to see the city as Hell—either the holy one of vision or the real
counterpart—in direct opposition to most modern writers, such as
Baudelaire, Eliot, Crane, and Joyce. In this sense he is almost unique.

Since his philosophical training was very heavily influenced by
Neoplatonics, Pound did not want to limit his concept of the ideal to a
social context. After the late 1930's, when he was finishing his basic
work on economics, he turned with renewed interest to mystical
works, even to the spiritualism of William Butler Yeats, a thing that
had previously troubled him gravely. He rediscovered men like John
Heydon, the forgotten seventeenth-century occultist, and delved into
little-read works like Philostratus' *Life of Apollonius of Tyana*, that
brilliant narration of the life of a Hellenic Messiah. It is hard to
imagine Ezra spending much time on Apollonius in the 1920's and
1930's, for he would have seen too much of the Hindu or the Buddhist
in the unheralded wise man.

After the purgative effect of the Pisan concentration camp, the
madhouse of St. Elizabeths seems to have almost magically transformed itself into a kind of monastery. Pound had many friends to
bring him books, and he finally had access to something that had
always been lacking in Rapallo: a magnificent reserve of scholarly
material, the Library of Congress. As a result, his homecoming was
not as bitter as it might have been. Out of the hellish atmosphere of the
asylum Pound was able to effect his own psychic redemption. He was
able to achieve high states of mind far removed from the chaos around
him, even though they did not last long: "but the mind as Ixion,
unstill, ever turning" (Canto 113/790).

Pound fully believed that the continuum of the mind will never
admit long periods of any one of the three states of mind that Dante
had carved into his canticles. This notion may well answer the criticism of the anti-Poundians who complain that there is no continuity in
the Later Cantos, that 85 and 86, which depend heavily on the *Shu
King* or *History Classic*, are placed at random next to 87 and 88,
where the American history of the age of Jackson predominates,
without any clearly marked correlation between the two units. The
negativists will hold that the social nature of most of *Rock-Drill* and
Thrones does not blend well with the mystical elements. How can we
go from the technical language of the *Code of Justinian* to snippets

from the *Life of Apollonius?* How can we relate the Del Mar lecture
on economics, which forms the underlying structure of Canto 97, to
the beautiful religious opening of Canto 98? Pound's answer might on
the one hand be: don't ask for continuity from an author who does not
prize it or even believe in it. On the other hand, we must again broach
the problem presented in Chapter 5 about the welding of Aristotelian
and Neoplatonic elements in Pound's philosophy, for the problem lies
here. Undoubtedly the arrangement of the Later Cantos tells us that
Pound does not feel that a problem of unity really exists. He indicates
that a rock-drill is necessary for the erection of thrones, thrones that
are both the seats of kings (and thus social in nature), but also
"something God can sit on/ without having it sqush" (Canto
88/581:616). Pound would ask: why separate your physics from your
metaphysics? Why can't the two be related? In fact, his admiration
for Confucius and Mencius lies precisely in the fact that he feels that
their philosophy is intimately bound up with the handling of religious
rites. There is no meta-physics, strictly speaking, in their world-
views, for nature is presented as an undifferentiated continuum.
Pound actually goes so far as to suggest that the same holds true for a
great deal of the best Occidental thought:

μετά τὰ φυσικά
    metah, not so extraneous, possibly not so extraneous
most *"metas"* seem to be in with.   (Canto 97/680:710)

Canto 98 is a good illustration of the way in which Pound builds
on the so-called *Sacred Edict* or *Sheng U* of Emperor K'ang Hsi in
order to establish ground rules for the construction of an ideal society. During the course of the canto, Pound lists all sixteen of the
points which the edict covered, usually in paraphrase and sometimes
obliquely. The canto ends with the mention of six rites for a festival,
thus linking the religious ceremony, which is tied in with nature, to
the social proclamation. The process is continued in Canto
99/695:725, where the religious rites and the "blue grass" of the
natural scene blend with a further spelling out of the sixteen points; it
contains the line: "To trace out and to bind together." Doubtlessly
Pound is using the justifiable etymology which analyzes the Latin
word *religio* as a composite of *re-* (again, together) and *ligo* (bind).

Religion is the instrument for binding all things together, including those of ostensibly lower orders. To invert the idea, a social paradise is a necessary prelude for a lasting psychic one. If we are thinking in terms of perfection, we must bind nature, society, and the individual psyche into an ideogrammic relationship where whatever is said of the one must relate to the other. As Pound himself says at the close of the canto:

> The fu jen receives heaven, earth, middle
>   and grows.

Actually the design of the Later Cantos must become apparent to anyone who reads them with a sincere attempt to give them their due. Granted that they are full of many apparently arbitrary details and that the language in them is sometimes clipped, still we can see that this section is comparable with the last work of a Mozart. The Later Cantos show a fusion of many of the ideas that Pound had introduced in the earlier portions of the poem. The Kung of Canto 13 merges with Mencius fully as the voice of human reason in the sphere of social conduct. Cantos 85 and 86 reinforce the lesson of the earlier Chinese Cantos: that justice and peace were attained only in dynasties that followed Confucian precepts. Cantos 88 and 89 continue the work of the Jefferson and Adams Cantos, presenting the administrations of Jackson and Van Buren largely as seen through the pages of Thomas Hart Benton's *Thirty Years' View*. These cantos are all of the true rock-drill type, for they deal with the forging of a paradise as a political entity. Canto 90, by contrast, presents the heaven of pure contemplation, the place of beautiful women, ocular apprehension, prayer, and love:

> out of Erebus, the deep-lying
>   from the wind under the earth,
>   m'elevasti
> from the dulled air and the dust,
>   m'elevasti,
> by the great flight,
>   m'elevasti
>   Isis Kuanon
>   from the cusp of the moon,
>   m'elevasti   (606:640)

The Italian phrase (you raised me) is modeled after Dante's *mi levasti* of *Paradiso* I.75, which the poet directs lovingly to Beatrice. We might say that the balanced state of mind in Canto 90, in Pound's view, can exist only upon the foundation of the preceding parts of the work. Similarly, in Canto 94 the Messiah of love Apollonius rises out of the ordered world of Rome. Unlike Christ, whom Pound constantly badgered for being unpolitical, Apollonius was concerned with the Empire's effect on Greece; he lectured Vespasian and thus helped to prepare the road for the overthrow of Nero. It is no wonder, then, that next to some lovely paraphrases of Philostratus' Greek, which describe Apollonius riding up the Nile in his barge or communicating with seals, tigers, and leopards, we have the rock-like legal language upon which the Roman and Byzantine Empires were founded.

The influence of Alexander del Mar is quite apparent in the *Thrones* section of the poem, where Pound discovers Byzantium. Del Mar claimed in his *History of Monetary Systems* that Byzantium's standard silver-gold ratio of 12 to 1 and its equitable rates of interest sustained the impressive millennial sweep of its empire. He thus supplied economic grounds for asserting the might and the majesty of an empire that Pound had admired for other reasons: Neoplatonism, which may rightfully be regarded as one of the primary heritages of the Byzantine Empire, and Byzantine or Romanesque art and architecture. After reading Del Mar, Pound had the final period to place between his America of Adams and the Greco-Roman past. The Italian Renaissance thus becomes largely ignored in the Later Cantos; instead, Byzantium moves in as the heir to the greatness of Greece and Rome and the direct progenitor of what is most salvageable for the present. Not curiously, Dante is seen as the Roman or western end-product of the Byzantine development. Instead of regarding Dante as a pre-Renaissance realist and kinsman of Aquinas, Pound views him as a member of that fraternity of Neoplatonic nature disciples who preached love in the Apollonian tradition, with a strong dash of Aristotelian logic in his social thinking and classical precision in his words.

While Pound is bringing his Ancient-Medieval-Modern phases of history into focus, he is also doing something else that he has done before in the poem: linking the Greek (now the Byzantine Greek) with the Chinese, for Pound feels that these two cultures furnish the cornerstones for all that is permanent in human endeavor, standing against the ravages of the Mongols, Moguls, Tartars, Cazars, Avars, Gepids, and the other tribes that roll off the pages of *Thrones*.

Pound scatters his Chinese characters throughout Canto 96, which presents the early history of the Lombards (admirable lawgivers under Rothar and his successors), the history of Byzantine rulers after Constantine, and finally the *Edict of the Eparch*, a decree issued by Leo the Wise (ruled 886-912). For example, we have a direct correlation of the Greek words in the edict with some Chinese that runs in the right column of page 659:690. The *Edict* itself lays down the laws for merchants and tradesmen in clear, concise language. Pound likes the precision so much that he is constantly commenting on individual words in a way that makes the word of the lord seem almost the Logos itself.

The canto that follows gives us Del Mar's yoking of the Chinese and Byzantine systems as prime samples of achievement. In Cantos 98 and 99, a fusion occurs, for here Pound pulls K'ang Hsi's *Sacred Edict* into alignment with the decree of Leo the Wise. He thus accomplishes poetically what Del Mar does discursively. Not infelicitously for this study, Dante becomes one of the ways in which the two worlds are bound together, as, for example:

> Sixteen bitched by an (%) interest rate
> Byzantium rather more durable
>   "from rib to cheek whose palate cost so dear"
> Miss Mitford (or one-ov'um) thought this was "gothic"
>   Paradiso, XIV: this light does not dis-unify.   (98/692:722)

Pound is stating that the sixteen rules of the *Sacred Edict* were ineffective because the interest rates set by the government were too high. Ahead on page 684:714 we learn that the interest rate in Byzantium was "12% for a millennium," whereas "The Manchu at 36 legal," as the *Sacred Edict* itself admits (ed. Baller, pp. 32 f.). The lines cited above show a linking of the economic statement with art: a durable kingdom creates a vital art that is "dear"; we then have a mistaking of Romanesque beauty for Gothic—a thing that causes horror to Pound, who sees the Gothic as a barbaric counterpoint to the Mediterranean sense of symmetry and balance. What connects the art and the money and the beauty is a reference to *Paradiso* XIII.55 f., where Dante says that "this living light . . . does not disunify" (Pound cites Canto XIV to show the general use of the conceit; on the next page he cites Canto

XIII correctly for the direct quotation). In the Confucian commentaries, Pound had seen the sun and light as a radical of the characters relating to virtue, intelligence, and justice. Similarly, Dante's *Paradiso* can be treated as a "coming into light," as can Plotinus' *Enneads* and Scotus' *De divisione naturae*. Dante thus acts as a literary focal point between the splendid mosaics of Byzantium and the shining knowledge of China. Could we not almost say that Pound considers Dante the son of the Byzantine tradition, since that Empire never produced the culminating epic that its western brother did?

It is no accident that Pound puts the phrase "volgar' eloquio" (popular speech) on page 686:716 next to the characters representing the name Iu-p'uh. The original edict of K'ang Hsi had been written concisely to the point of being unintelligible, and was partially edited by Yong Tching, his son, who appears in Canto 61. It was then elaborated upon in a popular idiom by Ouang-iu-p'uh (as Pound transcribes the name) in a way that made it accessible to all. Pound sees a connection here between Dante, who elected to write in Italian out of his love for the people and his desire to educate them; the allusion refers not only to the *De vulgari eloquio* (which was ironically written in Latin), but to the *Convivio* and the *Comedy* itself. The Later Cantos are very much concerned with the love that supplies the form for philosophy. Dante is, in Pound's eyes, an important part of this tradition of sages who work for the welfare of the people, as opposed to those who pander to the taste of oligarchs and aristocrats.

Direct allusions to the *Paradiso* abound in the Later Cantos. These include a few mentions of characters. For example, Piccarda Donati, who appears in *Paradiso* III, is cited briefly in Canto 93/628:661, where she is merely grouped as Cunizza was with other beautiful ladies. The heretic Sigier of Brabant, whom Dante undauntedly included among orthodox thinkers in his Heaven of the Sun, is cited in Canto 107/756:781: " 'that light which was Sigier' ", but the reference seems to be more to the light than to Sigier, as is shown in the lines that follow. Likewise the reference to the troubadour-become-bishop Folquet of Marseille in Canto 92/619:652 seems to be pinpointing the light *(lumera)* of the Third Heaven, where Folquet appears, rather than to be referring to Folquet as a distinct historical personality:

> "in questa lumera appresso"
>
>   Folquet, nel terzo cielo.

"And if I see her not,
no sight is worth the beauty of my thought."

Similarly the phrase "scala altrui" (another man's stair) in Canto 113/790, a reference to Cacciaguida's prophecy that Dante would have to learn how to climb another man's staircase, is almost parenthetically cited after a sentimental catalogue of vanishing things:

A blue light under stars.
The ruined orchards, trees rotting. Empty frames at Limone.
And for a little magnanimity somewhere,
And to know the share from the charge
(scala altrui)
God's eye art 'ou, do not surrender perception.

There is a suggestion here of the pathos, the sense of struggle and loss, that characterizes Cacciaguida's talk, but it is not insisted upon. As we have seen in his handling of Cunizza in the preceding chapter, Pound treated Dante's paradisal characters as examples of ideas, almost as symbolic images, precisely as Dante himself did in his final canticle.

Therefore to reconstruct Pound's use of the Italian, we must focus on the modern writer's handling of philosophy. In so doing, we must move away from the *Paradiso* to the *Convivio*, that much-neglected philosophical work that Dante himself abandoned, a work that appealed greatly to Pound during his incarceration in St. Elizabeths. In his handbook *Dante*, Francis Fergusson spells out the importance of the *Convivio* in the subtitle of his third chapter: "Dante's Cult of Reason, 1293-1308." More than any other twentieth-century critic, Fergusson was keenly aware of the relationship between Dante and the Greek philosopher, as when he makes the seminal equation: "For Dante, *amor* =the movement of the spirit toward what it perceives as pleasant or good= 'action' (in Aristotle's terms)" (p. 50). Pound repeatedly expresses this movement as the *directio voluntatis* or "direction of the will"; he in effect makes the *voluntas* or will almost equal *voluptas* or desire. The Latin term beloved by Pound is fully applicable to the volitionist tendencies of the *Convivio* as a whole. In Canto 87/572:608 Pound puts the Latin phrase under the character *chih*[4], 志, which means "aim, intention," and later he expands his application as follows:

Justice, directio voluntatis
  or contemplatio as Richardus defined it in Benjamin Major.

(Canto 87/576:612)

Acts of cognition, acts of implementing virtue, and acts of love
are all co-related in Pound's mind. Most Dantistas will acknowledge
that the same holds true for the Italian. Without love there can be no
justice, and without love there can be no true knowledge, as is stated
in Canto 77/467:497:

Their aims as one
directio voluntatis, as lord over the heart
    the two sages united

Many medievalists would align Dante with St. Thomas Aquinas,
but Pound balks at this coupling. He sees Dante working in a tradition
that has its roots in Aristotle, but one that proliferates through those
Neoplatonics who resisted hypermysticism on the one hand and arid
Scholasticism on the other; it was a tradition that retained some sense
of love and respect for nature, as he insists in Canto 85/546:582:

Dante, out of St Victor (Richardus),
  Erigena with greek tags in his verses.

In Canto 87/570:606, he employs the tripartite Neoplatonic stages of
cognition:

"Cogitatio, meditatio, contemplatio."
  Wrote Richardus, and Dante read him.

The love element is present in almost all of the Neoplatonics from
Plotinus through St. Francis of Assisi. It is too little apparent in the
opposite tradition, as shows in the rigid picture of St. Dominic given
by St. Bonaventure in *Paradiso* XII.

To return to the *Convivio,* which adds rational philosophic commentaries to poems of the heart, we can spell out at least three major
statements of the work:

1. Love is insisted upon as the perfect operation of the human organism.
2. What is said of individuals is fully applicable to societies.
3. Nobility is the name of the virtue which emanates from love; it cannot be attained by blood ties or money.

Point 1 is established in several places in the *Convivio*, but nowhere more eloquently than in the First Canzone, where Love is called the "true lord" *(segnor verace,* line 51) and in the commentary that follows. Pound seizes on this idea in Canto 93/626:659, which might almost be called the Dante Canto:

> That love is the "form" of philosophy,
> is its shape (è forma di Filosofia)
> and that men are naturally friendly
>   at any rate from his (Dant's) point of view
> tho' he puts knowledge higher than I should
> and, elsewhere: "her" beltà,
>   cioè moralitade,
> rains flakes of fire,"
>   but is not speaking of knowledge.

This is a general amalgam of several Dantesque passages, most notably the entire commentary in *Convivio* III, where Lady Philosophy is taken as the woman loved by the poet and in turn bestowing love upon him; the statement that "Love is the form of Philosophy" is made at III.xiii.10. The rain of fire occurs in the canzone before the commentary in line 63: *Sua bieltà piove fiammelle di foco* (Her beauty rains down flakes of fire). The idea "that men are naturally friendly" is stated in *Convivio* I.i: *ciascuno uomo a ciascuno uomo naturalmente è amico.* This concept is compressed in the general phrase *compagnevole animale,* which means "companionable, friendly animal" or also "social animal," as is clear when Dante mentions Aristotle as his source in *Convivio* IV.iv: *E però dice lo Filosofo che l'uomo naturalmente è compagnevole animale* (And thus the Philosopher says that man is naturally a friendly animal). Pound places the Italian phrase in 93/626:659, beside the hieroglyph that he associates with the Egyptian king Kati (Khaty). It occurs again in Canto 95/643:676:

> "Not political," Dante says, a
>   "compagnevole animale"
> Even if some do coagulate into cities
>   πόλις, πολιτική

Pound does not want us to interpret Aristotle's *politike* as "political"; a few lines later he connects the Greek work with the verb *poleuo,* "to plow," thereby underscoring the pastoral qualities of the connotation, as against the smoke-filled rooms of cities.

As we can see from our discussion, point 1 above leads quite naturally to point 3, for a man in love will radiate not only the emotion, the physical *virtus*, but also the moral virtue that proceeds from it. As Pound says in Canto 93/626:659; " 'onestade risplende.' Dio, la prima bontade" (Honor or honesty shines. God, the first goodness). These fragments occur in the *Convivio*'s Third Canzone from line 121 onward:

> The soul which is adorned by this goodness
> never holds it concealed in her,
> for from the principle which is wedded to her body,
> she manifests it to her death.
> Obedient, gentle, and modest
> she is in her first age,
> and her person is adorned with beauty . . .

> *L'anima cui adorna esta bontate*
> *non la si tiene ascosa,*
> *chè dal principio ch'al corpo si sposa*
> *la mostra infin la morte.*
> *Ubidente, soave e vergognosa*
> *è ne la prima etate,*
> *e sua persona adorna di bieltate . . .*

They are picked up in the commentary that follows in IV.xxv.11 ff. and are also stated in III.xv.11:

> Whereby one should know that morality is the beauty of philosophy; for just as bodily beauty results from the members being rightfully placed, so the beauty of wisdom, which is the body of philosophy, . . . results from the ordering of the moral virtues, which make this pleasure felt sensibly. And so I say that her beauty—that is, morality—rains down flakes of fire.

> *Dove è da sapere che la moralitade è bellezza de la filosofia; chè così come la bellezza del corpo resulta da le membra in quanto sono debitamente ordinate, così la bellezza de la sapienza, che è corpo di Filosofia, . . . resulta da l'ordine de le virtudi morali, che fanno quella piacere sensibilmente. E però dico che sua biltà, cioè moralitade, piove fiammelle di foco.*

Pound draws the social implications from this passage in Canto 93/627:660:

> and mentions distributive justice, Dante does, in Convivio
>   Four, eleven
> "cui adorna esta bontade" . . .

Indeed *Convivio* IV.xi.6 does contain the phrase *distributiva giustizia*, and the social ramifications of the words, which spring from the psychology of the individual, are never forgotten. Both the Second and the Third Canzoni of the *Convivio* seem to have blended in Pound's mind, and indeed the fusion is not incorrect, for what is said of the good operation of a soul in love can be said equally well of a loving society, as was noted in point 2 above. It is a Neoplatonic tenet that there is never a dearth of love from loving, for love is not a material object like a pie, and therefore it is not diminished as it is distributed. Love is increased through distribution, like all things spiritual, including light, or the bread of angels, the *panis angelicus* of Canto 93/623:656, which Dante promises to distribute among his readers in *Convivio* I.i. We can all share the feast of wisdom, where the bounty is ever flowing. But the spiritual notion for Pound must also be pragmatic, for his metaphysic is never entirely divorced from his concerns for politics or for ethics, any more than it is in Dante. That is why Ezra puts the name of the good Egyptian aristocrat Antef next to the Dantesque quotation on page 623:656: it underscores the social application of the metaphysical rule, for Antef distributed bread as well as love among his people. Andy Jackson wanted wealth in the pants of the people, and

> . . . T'ang opened the copper mine
> (distributive function of money).   (Canto 88/580:616)

Pound uses "bread" in the social communal sense, as well as in the religious communional, but without a Christlike application: the wheat is produced through hard work and attention to the soil, not by miracles.

The doctrine of love as the never-ending "bread of the spiritual life" is beautifully stated by Vergil (how Reason apprehends!) in a longish passage in *Purgatorio* XV.46 ff. It is repeated in an abbreviated form in *Paradiso* V.105, with the cry "Look! here is one who will increase our loves!" (*"Ecco chi crescerà li nostri amori"*), which is uttered by every one of the souls who approach Dante in the sphere of Mercury. Pound picks up the line in Canto 89/590:625, and in 116/796, using it perhaps to the fullest advantage in 93/631:664:

> E "chi crescerà" they would be individuals.
> Swedenborg said "of societies"
>   by attraction.

Emanuel Swedenborg is used to expand the notion outward—a typical centrifugal development in Pound's poetry.

The importance of man's social nature is spelled out again and again in the *Cantos* and in the *Convivio*. Dante remarks in IV.xxvii.3: "as Aristotle says, man is a social or political animal" *(sì come Aristotile dice, l'uomo è animale civile)*. In *Paradiso* VIII, Charles Martel, who died in 1294 but knew Dante well enough to cite the opening line of the First Canzone of the *Convivio* upon meeting him, is discoursing with the pilgrim about a variety of topics, one of them being the apparent disparity between the talents of people, a disparity which does not correspond with the absolutely equitable way in which the heavens operate. He says abruptly at line 115:

> "But tell me—would it be worse
> for man on earth, if he wasn't a citizen?"

> *"Or dì: sarebbe il peggio*
> *per l'omo in terra, se non fosse cive?"*

Dante has to reply: yes. Charles goes on to explain the disparity by saying that we mortals are too far removed from Perfect Intelligence to operate with perfection. This is in a sense another statement of the Fortuna theme, that everything under the moon is imperfect.

But given this inequitable social base, man must strive for justice, even though at times the attainment of it seems impossible. Dante uses the ancient Roman Cato almost as a symbol for the concept in *Purgatorio* I.42, where he speaks about the man "moving his honest feathers" like some proud bird: *movendo quelle oneste piume*. Pound, who was very much concerned with the workings of justice during his confinement in St. Elizabeths, picks up Cato in Canto 86/565:601, and mentions the "Honest feathers" in Canto 96/664:695. He gives us a tiny capsule of the birth of philosophy through Pythagoras in Canto 93/626:658:

> In the time of Numa Pompilius
>   che Pitagora si chiamò.
> "non sempre" (in the 3rd of Convivio)
> or as above stated "jagged"
> l'amor che ti fa bella

These elliptical allusions depend first of all upon *Convivio* III.xi.3:

> . . . almost at the time of Numa Pompilius, second king of the Romans, there lived a very noble philosopher, who was called Pythagoras.
>
> *. . . nel tempo quasi che Numa Pompilio, secondo re de li Romani, vivea uno filosofo nobilissimo, che si chiamò Pittagora.*

The verse establishes the foundation of philosophy concurrently with a strong kingship that paved the way for the Roman Empire. Pound (and Dante?) suggests that there is a correlation between the two. Pound's "non sempre" (not always) appears in *Convivio* III.xiii.3:

> I say therefore that people who are in love here, that is: in this life, feel it (intelligence) in their thought, not always but when Love makes his peace felt.
>
> *Dico adunque che la gente che s'innamora 'qui', cioè in questa vita, la sente nel suo pensiero, non sempre, ma quando Amore fa de la sua pace sentire.*

Philosophy is connected with the emotions here, and the notion that tranquility is a paradisal state of mind achieved through love and the intellect is clearly expressed, although, as Pound notes again, the duration is "jagged." Philosophy thus becomes a sentient thing, as Cavalcanti had presented it. Pound further makes Dante subscribe to his own belief that heaven is a condition of mind; as the Egyptian Kati says at the opening of Canto 93: "A man's paradise is his good nature." The last statement from the Canto 93 citation means "the love that makes you beautiful," and is taken from *Convivio* III.xiii.9.

The regenerative power of intellectual love, leading to a "new life," was Dante's central theme in the *Vita Nuova*. Love redeems, as well as sustains. This idea is also central to Pound's thinking, as he shows in Canto 93/630:663, when he writes the words "nuova vita" under the character *hsien*,[3] 顯 which means "show, appear" as a verb and "glorious, manifest" as an adjective. Next come the Italian words "e ti fiammeggio" (and I flame, glow for you), which is what Beatrice says in *Paradiso* V.1 as she illuminates the mind of her lover and enlightens his eyes. Pound constantly relates this concept of renovation to the Confucian idea of renewal through learning and action, as in Canto 93/629:662:

"Renew"

as on the T'ang tub:

Renew

jih   日

hsin   新

renew

Plus the luminous eye

見   chien⁴

These words harken back to Canto 53/264:274, where we learned that "Tching prayed on the mountain and/ wrote MAKE IT NEW/ on his bath tub." The *hsin*¹ *jih*⁴ characters appear to the right, with some punctuation marks inadvertently added by Dorothy in her brushwork (see Kenner's *Pound Era*, p. 448). On page 629:662 they are related to the eyes and knowledge, with the stress on the empirical nature of learning and spiritual radiance. Since the character *hsin*¹ consists of an axe clearing out weeds, it can be further related to Dante's use of *novelle piante* (new plants) to replace the old in *Purgatorio* XXXIII.143. We thus see Dante and Confucius blending in matters imagistic as well as conceptual.

The eyes and light, in fact, dominate Canto 93, just as they permeate the *Paradiso*. Pound almost seems to see the entire personality in terms of light, as in Canto 107/756:781:

Light, cubic
            by volume
    so that Dante's view is quite natural;
            (Tenth, Paradiso, nel Sole)

or again on page 762:787, where the Dante-Confucius correspondence is spelled out, in company with a Neoplatonic philosopher, an English lawgiver, and an American scientist:

So that Dante's view is quite natural:
            this light
                    as a river
        in Kung; in Ocellus, Coke, Agassiz
                    ρεῖ, the flowing
                    this persistent awareness

The Greek word means "flows," as in *panta rhei* (all things flow), and serves to connect the light and the river. The Later Cantos are bathed in words of love, just as they are resplendent with light—the two going naturally together. The *terzo cielo* (third heaven) mentioned in Canto 91/617:650 is, properly speaking, the locus for the entire last third of the poem. For Love as the great dictator (Dante's *ch'e' ditta dentro* of *Purgatorio* XXIV) is cited in Canto 85/552:588, and the warm, flowing movement of the later cantos of the *Paradiso* is captured in lines such as these from Canto 91/611:645:

> Light *compenetrans* of the spirits
> The Princess Ra-Set has climbed
>   to the great knees of stone,
> She enters protection,
>   the great cloud is about her,
> She has entered the protection of crystal
>   convien che si mova
>   la mente, amando
>   XXVI, 34

Here Pound sees the whole universal turning as an act of love, precisely as Dante did, with the outer stretches of the protective Crystalline Heavens mentioned. The Italian lines, taken from *Paradiso* XXVI.34-35, mean "It is right that the mind should move by loving." At this point the words seem as much Pound's as Dante's.

We can see as we proceed through the Later Cantos how Pound in fact becomes Dante, who in turn takes on much of the form of the great sage of China. All three personalities by the end of the *Cantos* are inextricably interwoven. The sage delights in water, in joy, in tranquility, and in Canto 100/716:743, Pound again cites Dante's *Paradiso* (XVIII.42) in a context of social joy and grace abounding:

> Barley, rice, cotton, tax-free
>   with hilaritas.
> Letizia, Dante, Canto 18   a religion
> *Virtù* enters.
>   Buona da sè volontà.   (*Will good by itself*)
> Lume non è, se non dal sereno   (*No light if not from the serene*)
>   stone to stone, as a river descending
> the sound a gemmed light,
>   form is from the lute's neck.

As early as Canto 39/194:202 Pound had spoken of celestial joy, using first a somewhat misquoted line from *Paradiso* XXIII.129: "Che mai da me non si parte il diletto" (so that never does the delight part from me) and one from XXX.62: "Fulvida di folgore" (dazzling with lightning; the *fulvido* of most texts is sometimes emended to *fulgido*, "resplendent," or *fluvido-fluido*, "flowing"—this last preserving the water imagery). Both allusions describe the light of Heaven, and both were somewhat pedantic, like many of the Dantesque brushstrokes Pound employed in the Early Cantos. In his old age, Pound used the Florentine in a way that brings the admirer of Dante as much surprise as delight. For example, one of the most formidable passages in the *Comedy* occurs in *Paradiso* XXIV.64ff., where Dante is defining faith for St. Peter in order to enter the gates of Heaven:

> "Faith is the substance of things hoped for,
> and the proof of things not apparent,
> and this I take to be its quiddity."

> *"fede è sustanza di cose sperate*
> *e argomento de le non parventi;*
> *e questa pare a me sua quiditate."*

One can read this passage a hundred times in the Italian and see only an arid Scholastic definition here. But when one sees Pound's adaptation of the puzzling word *quiditate*, as in Canto 89/600:635, he pauses and considers:

> Wright spoke to mind not to passions and
> he it was brought in Polk.
> Quiditas, remarked D. Alighieri.

Suddenly we are forced to rethink Dante, to see that the "faith" he is talking about is a very dynamic thing that depends upon ideals, not upon actualization. The proposition is firmly volitionist and active: faith is something that one must constantly create. The concept springs to life with renewed vigor, and this vigor can be translated by Pound into poetry of the highest order:

> "A spirit in cloth of gold"
>   so Merlin's moder said,
> or did not say,

```
        left the quidity
             but remembered
& from fire to crystal
        via the body of light,
           the gold wings assemble        (Canto 91/615:648)
```

Faith is substantial, is a part of the what-ness of the perfectly realized human creature. Only in the last moments of ascension to the purely spiritual can it be put aside, or not so much put aside as used as a fulcrum for transcendence.

In the madhouse in Washington the Italian master stepped down out of his books and lent a hand to the man who more than any other over the last 700 years had heeded his every word and had tried to "make him new." The figure of the Italian sage—whether the benign Dante of Botticelli or the magic Dante of the medievalists—was certainly the kind of man whom Pound envisaged during those troubled days. The Dante of fire and brimstone and tirades on usury never disappeared; he merely yielded to the more tranquil figure, who stands in the great tradition of Apollonius of Tyana and Confucius. It was this persona that Pound himself finally adopted—a man whose vision was broad, whose perception was acute, whose ability to correlate was uncanny, and finally, whose capacity to love was unimpeded by ideas. In his later years, Pound became almost totally silent. But he had had his say. Now like the sages of Florence and China, he belonged to history.

10

ON JUDGING THE JUDGES

Dante has stood the test of time. He weathered his own turbulent age, when his many enemies tried to block him from achieving a peaceful later life and gaining the acclaim that he deserved. He lasted through the medieval-hating Age of Enlightenment, and really came into his own in the nineteenth and twentieth centuries. Despite the fact that our own time is not a great religious era, we look to him with far more veneration than his own age did. Pound might perhaps take comfort from Alighieri's fate, for the future could well produce a similar rise in the estimation of Ezra's work. Certainly the *Cantos* are not destined for early oblivion.

As for Dante, the *Comedy* finds a vigorous new audience in the young. Modern undergraduates, who retain very little interest in the dogma of the poem, are fascinated by its imagery and its movement toward pure spirituality—precisely the things that attracted Pound back in 1908. And of all the sensitive Dante critics, there is still none who has done a more thorough job in close reading of the text than Pound has. His *Spirit of Romance,* with its sensitivity to imagery, diction, and symbolism is still one of the best introductions to the *Comedy.* In one sense, Pound always veered a middle course in Dante criticism between the archly aesthetic position made famous by Benedetto Croce's *Poesia di Dante* and the rigidly religious readings of the modern apologists. Pound was close in spirit to Erich Auerbach, though he anticipated the scholar by a good 21 years. In his youth, Ezra always saw Dante as a "poet of the earthly world," with a strong emphasis on politics and reality. I suspect that this approach is still one of the best for the modern reader. Ezra's reading of the three canticles as "states of mind" rather than as transcriptions of actual events is probably the one adopted by most non-Catholic admirers of the work.

In Chapters 7 to 9 we saw the ways in which Dante assisted Pound: first, by lending color to the Poundian canvas or by casting a moral dimension over the work; secondly, by lending characters whom Pound could adopt as personae; and finally, by yielding his very psyche, which Pound seemed to assimilate in his final years. No "exchange" between two men could be completer. What was implied in "Scriptor Ignotus" is achieved in the Later Cantos. James Joyce's use of Homer in *Ulysses* is not in any sense comparable, for Joyce never becomes Homer himself; he merely uses Homeric materials.

It is now time to tackle the difficult question of Pound's success or failure in the *Cantos*. I believe quite simply that the work shows the century's strengths, as well as some of its weaknesses. Indeed, since Pound helped to carve the literature of the era, how could he remain aloof from the prevailing spirit? It might be helpful to attempt a comparison. Joyce, for example, can be said to have created a Hell in *Dubliners*, a Purgatory in *Ulysses,* and a Paradise in *Finnegans Wake*. In fact, Joyce's portrait of a modern Hell is penetrating dramatically, as Pound always admitted. But Ezra also wondered why anyone would want to spend the enormous effort required to unravel the prose of *Finnegans Wake* when all that he ends up with is a nightmare in the mind of a non-existent person. A deciphering of Pound's own difficult Later Cantos might at least lead one to a new social and political awareness. Pound believed with Rudolph Agricola that art is also supposed to instruct one morally. The *Wake* recedes inwardly to the subconscious and the unknowable, whereas the *Cantos* move outwardly to knowledge, action, and thought. If Joyce seems at times more universal than Pound, it is because he, like Jung, is working toward archetypes, ever probing into the unknown. Ezra, by contrast, resembles Freud (whom he detested), since he tries to wrench the mystery into a knowable form; he tries to bring the darkness into light.

One of the most frequent attacks launched against Pound is the lack of form in the *Cantos*. If the remarks in this book have any validity, certainly this argument cannot carry the weight that it did in the 1920's and 1930's when the overall design of the poem was not yet clear. There are two major kinds of form apparent in the *Cantos*, both of which have been discussed extensively here:

1. *Philosophic form:* the work has a tripartite organization which is based on the Victorine modes of cognition: cogitation, meditation, and contemplation; these movements form a vague analogue with Dante's Hell, Purgatory, and Paradise, but they are not in any sense fixed; they are constantly shifting. That is why the poem does not have a real ending. It trails off, the way music often does, because there is, strictly speaking, no end to the mind's movement until death. When Pound says in Canto 117/802 that he failed because he had tried to establish an Earthly Paradise, he was wrong not only about the nature of art (poems do not establish anything except states of mind in the readers), but also in underestimating his own achievement. His Adamsian America, his Leopoldine Siena, and his China of the T'angs are unforgettable. But the Pound of Canto 117 was a tired man who had been fighting entrenched enemies too long.

2. *Temporal and geographic form:* Distinctions of time and place are usually obliterated in the poem, despite the specificity of diction; all cities tend ultimately to become The City, although some surface individuality is retained. The active mind blurs arbitrary distinctions of matter: "How is it far if you think of it?" Still, perceptible chunks of history emerge and are fixed upon as centers of meditation to be gathered out of the void. These centers might be graphed as follows:

EAST

Three thousand years of Chinese history
****
Presiding genius: Confucianism

WEST

Ancient Greece-Rome	Byzantium	Ren. Italy	America
Aristotle	Neoplatonism	Dante	Adams-Pound

The poem very clearly realizes the dream of making East meet West, of singing the whole story of the tribe. It is not in any way as diffuse in its general form as people make it. Given the notion that the mind is the medium, and that the mind is an ever-shifting entity, we cannot expect neatly cut blocks and catalogues.

There will, of course, be those who deny the greatness of the *Cantos* on the grounds that they contain a great deal of bigotry and ill will. But can the same not be said of the *Comedy?* Would Pope

Boniface or Philip the Fair or Corso Donati have given Dante the
laurels that modern critics so willingly heap upon him? If by his death
Pound could still not win the Nobel Prize for Literature (or a lot of
lesser prizes), Dante would have had the same trouble in his own age.
One must remember that if a writer is going to presume to judge, he
must condemn, he must draw lines, he must necessarily hurt certain
people's feelings. These are the consequences of this genre that I
have called the "epic of judgement." Allegorical works can teach or
judge through abstractions, but the epic as defined by Dante and
Pound is grounded in individuals—and that's where the trouble lies.
One can only speculate that the passage of time will heal many of
these wounds.

Any charge that the *Cantos* represent a right-wing political
philosophy that is now defunct must be taken lightly. Fascism dies in
the *Cantos* in the concentration camp. Even when Ezra was most
caught up in the Mussolini movement, he always followed the lead of
Aristotle in keeping open the options for democracy: Jefferson and/or
Mussolini. The real political hero of the *Cantos* is John Adams, not
the Boss, and the real center of Pound's blazing interest is America,
even if most of his mature years in this country were spent in an
asylum. Pound is more liberal than his detractors make him. He was
one of the century's first campaigners for preserving the beauty of
nature, long before the word "ecology" was popular. His defense of
sex was accomplished far more intelligently than were those undertaken by Henry Miller and his followers. His accent on economics is
one that the America of the shrinking dollar is just beginning to
appreciate. And finally, his insistence on East-West concord seems to
have had a genuine political analogue in 1972 with the visit of Richard
Nixon to Peking. Pound's tragic error was his choice of Fascism in the
1920's; he paid for that error at Pisa and in Washington.

Of course there will always be some who do not believe in the
validity of an epic of judgement, who will say that didacticism and
personal judgements have no place in "true" poetry. This is perhaps
a matter of taste. These detractors might add further that Christ
himself said: "Judge not, that you be not judged. For with the judgement you pronounce you will be judged, and the measure you give
will be the measure you get." Dante in Verona and Pound in Pisa
might well have mulled over these words. But still, it seems to be
human nature to want to judge. It seems that every so many centuries

we perhaps need someone to review history for us, to show us where we are or perhaps where we are not. Pound assumed this enormous task and, given the extreme difficulties involved, did a better job than even he in his waning years was willing to grant.

All things considered, it is time to re-evaluate Pound's position in twentieth-century letters. It is time to stop congratulating him for inspiring other poets, for founding imagism, and for writing some lovely lyrics and trenchant satires. It is time to start complimenting him for his more obvious achievement: the writing of the most intellectually alive poem of the century.

SOME DANTE ALLUSIONS NOT MENTIONED IN THE TEXT

ch'intenerisce: Canto 74/431:457 *(Purg.* VIII.2)

"Deh! nuvoletta . . . ": Canto 29/144:149 *(Rime* No. 23, 1)

dove siede Peschiera: Canto 93/625:658 *(Inf.* XX.70)

e "d'udir . . . prode": Canto 93/626:659 *(Conv.* IV, Canz. III, 135)

e i cavalieri: Canto 90/608:642 *(Purg.* XIV.109)

"e solo in lealtà far si diletta": Canto 93/626:659 *(Conv.* IV, Canz. III, 131)

farfalla gasping: Canto 117/802 *(Purg.* x.125)

le donne e i cavalieri: Canto 20/95:99 *(Purg.* XIV.109)

si com' ad Arli: Canto 80/508:543 *(Inf.* IX.112)

NOTES TO CHAPTER 1

[1] See *Letters*, p. 180: "I am perhaps didactic; so in a sense, or in different senses are Homer, Dante, Villon, and Omar."

[2] Primary modern sources: N. Zingarelli, *Dante* (Milan, 1909), *La Vita, i tempi e le opere di Dante*, 3d ed. (Milan, 1931); shorter versions by T. G. Bergin, *Dante* (N. Y., 1965); Umberto Cosmo, *Handbook to Dante Studies*, tr. D. Moore (Oxford, 1950); Michele Barbi, *Life of Dante*, tr. P. G. Ruggiers (Berkeley, 1954).

[3] Early details summarized in the popular, often hypothetical account of Thomas C. Chubb, *Dante and His World* (Boston, 1966), pp. 10 ff.

[4] *Dante's Lyric Poetry*, ed. Foster-Boyde, *1*, 148-153.

[5] For indebtedness, see Zingarelli, *Dante*, p. 155; Boccaccio, *Vita di Dante* XXV, ed. C. Muscetta (Rome, 1963), p. 43.

[6] *Vita di Dante* V, p. 10.

[7] Barbi, pp. 9 f.

[8] Discussed by Bergin, *Dante*, pp. 31 ff.

[9] Giovanni Villani, *Cronica* VIII.13.

[10] Villani, *Cronica* V-VII; summarized by Barbi, pp. 9 ff.

[11] Recounted by Compagni, *Cronica* I.22 ff.

[12] *Vita di Dante* XI, p. 20.

[13] *Vita di Dante* III, p. 9, putting the visit in Dante's old age; Bruni, *Life of Dante* in *Divina Commedia*, tr. Henry Boyd, 3 vols. (London, 1802), *1*, 83; Villani, IX.136.

[14] *Life of Dante*, p. 20; but cf. Boccaccio, *Vita di Dante* XXVI, p. 51, who puts the *De vulgari "già vicino alla sua morte."* Dating problem much debated; possibly, like Pound's criticism, the work was written early and revised after poetic experience.

[15] Bruni, pp. 82-83.

[16] *Cronica* IX.136, dating the death in July.

[17] *Vita di Dante* XV-XVI, pp. 23 ff.; Bruni, p. 85.

[18] P. 86.

[19] For biographical facts, see Noel Stock, *Life of E. P.*(N.Y., 1970); Charles Norman, *E. P.*, rev. ed. (N.Y. 1969); and Michael Reck, *E. P.: Close-Up* (N.Y., 1967).

[20] See *Letters*, pp. 3, 61, 99, 178, 255.

[21] Among them, Stock, pp. 41-43; Norman, p. 23.

[22] *Paris Review*, 28(1962), 36.

[23] *Thus to Revisit* (London, 1921), pp. 167 ff.; *Return to Yesterday* (N.Y. 1932), pp. 373 ff.

[24] *Letters of W. B. Yeats*, ed. Allan Wade (London: Hart-Davis, 1954), p. 543.

[25] For an expanded version, see "A Retrospect," *Essays*, pp. 3 ff., or "A Stray Document," *Make It New*, pp. 335 ff.

[26] *Paris Review*, 28 (1962), 32.

[27] Described in Norman, pp. 239 ff.; Stock, pp. 237 ff.

[28] Described vividly in Mary de Rachewiltz, *Discretions* (Boston, 1971), by far the most revealing attempt at an account of Pound's life.

[29] E. g., *Letters*, pp. 310 f., and esp. the one to Santayana, p. 331.

[30] *E. P. Broadcasts in Federal Communications Commission Transcripts of Short Wave Broadcasts: Rome, 1941-43*, Feb. 10, 1942, p. 1 et al.

[31] *Discretions*, pp. 184 ff.

[32] See Julien Cornell, *Trial of E. P.* (N.Y., 1966).

[33] *SatR*, *29* (March 16, 1946), 32 f.; also *29* (Feb. 9, 1946), 26 f.

[34] "Question of the Pound Award," *16* (1949), 512 ff.

[35] "Treason's Strange Fruit," *32* (June 11, 1949), 9 ff. Rebuttals: *Case Against the "Saturday Review of Literature"* . . . *by the Fellows in American Letters of the Library of Congress* . . . (Chicago, 1949); Archibald MacLeish, *Poetry and Opinion* (Urbana, Ill, 1950).

[36] Alan Levy, "E. P.'s Voice of Silence," *New York Times* (Jan. 9, 1972), Sec. 6, 14 ff.

NOTES TO CHAPTER 2

[1] *Kulch..r*, p. 249; "How To Read," *Essays*, pp. 28, 35; "The Renaissance," *Essays*, p. 217; *ABC of Reading*, pp. 44 f.

[2] J. H. Whitfield, *Dante and Virgil* (Oxford, 1949).

[3] Zingarelli, *Dante*, p. 134; cf. G. A. Scartazzini, *Companion to Dante*, tr. A. J. Butler (London, 1893), p. 384.

[4] Sensitively discussed by E. G. Parodi, *Poesia e storia nella "D. C."* (Naples, 1920), p. 302 *et al.*

[5] See rev. ed. C. H. Grandgent (Boston, 1933), p. 216. For Dante and classics in general, E. R. Curtius, *European Lit. and Latin Middle Ages*, tr. W. R. Trask (N. Y., 1953), pp. 348 ff.; Edward Moore, *Studies in Dante*, 1st Series (Oxford, 1896): Henry Osborn Taylor, *Medieval Mind*, 4th ed. (Cambridge, Mass., 1951).

[6] "How to Read," *Essays*, pp. 27 f.; *Letters*, p. 87.

[7] *ABC of Reading*, p. 45: "Dante makes all his acknowledgements to Virgil (having appreciated the best of him), but the direct and indirect effect of Ovid on Dante's actual writing is possibly greater than Virgil's."

[8] Many studies stress the similarities: T. S. Eliot, "Dante," *Selected Essays*, 2d ed. (N. Y., 1950), pp. 231-237, esp. p. 235.

[9] P. 121; see also the version in *V. N.*, tr. Mark Musa (rpt. Bloomington, Ind., 1962), pp. 12 f.

[10] In "Arnaut Daniel," *Essays*, pp. 109 ff., Pound emphasizes comparisons of Arnaut and Dante by sound-making, *melopoeia*. See Maurice Bowra, "Dante and Arnaut Daniel," *Speculum*, *27* (1952), 459 ff.; T. G. Bergin, "Dante's Provençal Gallery," *Diversity of Dante* (New Brunswick, 1969), pp. 87 ff.

[11] (Univ. Park, Pa., 1970), pp. 18, 25.

[12] *Dante: Poet of Secular World*, tr. R. Manheim (Chicago, 1961), pp. 24 ff.

[13] For relationships between Provence and Italy, Adolf Gaspary, *Die sicilianische Dichterschule des dreizehnten Jahrhunderts* (Berlin, 1878); Maurice Valency, *In Praise of Love* (N. Y., 1958), pp. 195 ff.

[14] Guido Guinizelli is usually taken as the father of the school: Dmitri Scheludko, "Guinizelli und der Neuplatonismus," *DVLG*, *12* (1934), 364 ff.

[15] I disagree with Natalino Sapegno, who finds the experience to be "almost religious" in his edition of *D.C.* (Milan, 1957), p. 669. Balanced discussion by Hugo Friedrich, *Epochen der italienischen Lyrik* (Frankfurt, 1964), pp. 52 ff.

[16] I take *ditta* to mean "dictate," but am well aware that *dictare* in Latin meant primarily "to poetize," as in *ars dictaminis* and German *dichten* (see below, n. 26). Two good editions of Dante's predecessors: *Poeti del Duecento*, ed. Gianfranco Contini, 2 vols. (Milan, 1960); *Rime della scuola siciliana*, ed. Bruno Panvini, 2 vols. (Florence, 1962-64):

[17] *Translations*, pp. 15 ff.; see esp. Sonnets I, III, VI, XX, XXI, XXVI.

[18] *Rime di Guittone d'Arezzo*, ed. Francesco Egidi (Bari, 1940); cf. the trickery of Nos. 12 and 13 with the tractate quality of 20; at his best, as in No. 19, he is, as Pound would have advised him to be, close to prose.

[19] Cf. *V. N.* XXV and *Spirit*, pp. 131 f., where Pound relates Dante's handling of rhetoric to Browning.

[20] Critical assessment by Karl Vossler, *Mediaeval Culture*, tr. W. C. Lawton, 2 vols. (rpt. N. Y., 1958), *2*, 164; exegetical approaches by Charles S. Singleton, *Essay on the "Vita Nuova"* (Cambridge, Mass., 1949); J. E. Shaw, *Essays on the "Vita Nuova"* (Princeton, 1929); Domenico de Robertis, *Libro della "V. N.,"* 2d ed. (Florence, 1970).

[21] See above, n. 20; De Sanctis, *History of Italian Literature*, tr. Joan Redfern, 2 vols. (rpt. N. Y., 1968), *1*, 62 f.

[22] *Essays*, pp. 295 and 211, which aligns Dante with Flaubert; *ABC of Reading*, p. 74. See Forrest Read, "Pound, Joyce, and Flaubert: The Odysseans," *New Approaches*, ed. Hesse, pp. 125 ff.

[23] N. Christoph de Nagy, "Pound and Browning," *New Approaches*, ed. Hesse, pp. 86 ff.; Warren Ramsey, "Pound, Laforgue, and Dramatic Structure," *CL, 3* (1951), 47 ff. Pioneering study, still useful, is Hugh Kenner, *Poetry of E. P.* (Norfolk, Conn., 1951), to be complemented by *Pound Era* (Berkeley, 1971); see also Baumann, Brooke-Rose, Davie, Dekker, Emery in Bibliog. Of special interest: Karl Malkoff, "Allusion as Irony: Pound's Use of Dante in 'Hugh Selwyn Mauberley,' " *MinnR, 7* (1967), 81 ff.

[24] However, for the valid concept of "Dante's *Purgatorio* as Elegy," see E. D. Blodgett, *The Rarer Action: Essays in Honor of Francis Fergusson*, ed. A. Cheuse and R. Koffler (New Brunswick, 1970), pp. 161 ff.

[25] Guinizelli text in *Poeti del Duecento*, ed. Contini, *2*, 460 ff.; for a full trans., see my *Medieval Song* (N. Y., 1971), p. 232.

[26] *ABC of Reading*, p. 36, where he relates German *dichten* to the word for "thickening." For my own explanation, see above, n. 16. On Dante's importance to imagism, see Giovanni Giovannini, *E. P. and Dante* (Utrecht, 1961), p. 8.

[27] *Dante*, pp. 50 f., 59; Joseph Anglade, *Les Troubadours*, 2d ed. (Paris, 1919), pp. 137 ff.

[28] *Translations*, p. 160. Scholarly edition by U. A. Canello, *La Vita e le opere del trovatore Arnaldo Daniello* (Halle, 1883); see Salvatore Battaglia, *Le Rime "petrose" e la sestina* (Naples, 1964).

[29] *Dante: Poet of Secular World*, p. 20; the German edition (Berlin, 1929) used *Vulgärspiritualismus* (p. 26), which would have been better translated as "secular mysticism," since the term is meant to be positive; I use the English rendition of the phrase here and elsewhere pejoratively.

[30] For studies of Pound's early poetry, see Jackson, De Nagy, Schneidau, Witemeyer, Ruthven, and Espey in Select Bibliography.
[31] Tr. in my *Seven Troubadors*, pp. 166 ff.

NOTES TO CHAPTER 3

[1] For Pound's assessment, see *Pound/Joyce*, ed. Read, pp. 228, 237, 239.
[2] *Mediaeval Culture, 1*, 154 f.; also, 153.
[3] *De divisione naturae* III: *Patrologia Latina*, ed. J. P. Migne, 221 vols. (Paris, 1844-1880), *122*, cols. 619 ff., for the created world of matter: see *Kulchur*, pp. 75, 77, 164 f., 333.
[4] It is useful to adhere to Scotus because of Pound's frequent use of him; see Walter B. Michaels, "Pound and Erigena," *Paideuma, 1* (1972), 37 ff.
[5] Howard Rollin Patch, *Tradition of Boethius* (N. Y., 1935), pp. 43 f., 121, etc.
[6] Charles S. Singleton, *Dante Studies 2: Journey to Beatrice* (Cambridge, Mass., 1958), pp. 122 ff.
[7] Seminal essay for allegorical interpretations: Erich Auerbach, "Figura," *Scenes from the Drama of European Literature* (N. Y., 1959), pp. 11 ff.; cf. Thomas M. Greene, "Dramas of Selfhood in the Comedy," *From Time to Eternity*, ed. T. G. Bergin, pp. 103 ff.
[8] See *Letters*, pp. 327 f., 331.
[9] *Companion to Dante*, p. 385.
[10] Maurice de Wulf, *History of Mediaeval Philosophy*, tr. E. C. Messenger, 3d ed. 2 vols. (London, 1935-38), *2*, 147: Thomas "surpassed Aristotle, inasmuch as he combined the naturalism of the latter with the idealism of Plato and Augustine, tempering and completing the one by the other."
[11] Whitfield, p. 73; Curtius, pp. 59 ff.
[12] Harold H. Watts, *E. P. and "Cantos"* (Chicago, 1952); Noel Stock, *Poet in Exile* (Manchester, 1964), pp. 121 ff.
[13] *Paris Review, 28*, 23.
[14] *De praedestinatione: Patrologia Latina, 122*, cols. 347-439. Cf. De Wulf, *1*, 121 ff.
[15] *Lustra* (N. Y., 1917), pp. 179 ff.; see the acid criticism of Yvor Winters, *Anatomy of Nonsense* (Norfolk, Conn., 1943), p. 160.
[16] For this troubled time, see Stock, *Life*, pp. 219 ff.
[17] Canto 40, pp. 199-201. See George Dekker, *Sailing After Knowledge* (London, 1963), pp. 35 ff.; Walter Baumann, *Rose in the Steel Dust* (Coral Gables, Fla., 1970), pp. 55 ff.
[18] See Clark Emery, *Ideas Into Action* (Coral Gables, Fla., 1958), pp. 5 ff.; on form, pp. 95 ff., with the analogue to Stravinsky on p. 96. Note remarks in *Confucius*, p. 95; *Kulchur*, pp. 15 ff., 127, 272 ff.
[19] *Intelligence of Louis Agassiz*, ed. Guy Davenport (Boston, 1963); see Canto 113, p. 786. For Erigena, *Kulchur*, pp. 75, 333; Canto 36, p. 179. Source: *De div. nat.*

I.66 *(P. L. 122*, col. 511): *"Vera enim auctoritas rectae rationi non obsistit, neque recta ratio verae auctoritati"*; also, I.64, 69.

[20] Guy Davenport, "Pound and Frobenius," *Motive and Method in "Cantos" of E. P.*, ed. Lewis Leary (N. Y., 1954), pp. 33 ff.

[21] As in Canto 4/16:20: "And we sit here . . ./ there in the arena". Or perhaps in a square, as in Venice, Canto 3/11:15.

[22] *Discretions*, pp. 111 f.; Canto 116/796.

[23] (Dublin: Cuala, 1929), rpt. in *A Vision*, rev. ed. (London: Macmillan, 1962), p. 4.

[24] Ibid., pp. 4 f.

[25] Unpublished Ph. D. thesis: "Reading of I-XXX of the 'Cantos' of E. P." (Harvard, 1961). See discussion by Pearlman, pp. 293 ff.

[26] *Paris Review, 28,* 48 f.

[27] Text: *Patrologia Latina, 196: De gratia contemplationis, sive Benjamin Major,* esp. I.3 (col. 66): *"De contemplationis proprietate, vel in quo differat a meditatione, vel cogitatione"*; Pound usually credits the *Benjamin Minor* (cols. 1 ff.). See *Selected Writings on Contemplation,* tr. Clare Kirchberger (London, 1957), p. 138, with note. De Wulf *(1,* 217) prefers Hugh of St. Victor as source; see Brooke-Rose, p. 33. Note the comment in Giovannini, pp. 8 f., that Pound spoke even in his Hamilton days of planning an epic in three parts: "the first in *terzine,* having to do with emotion . . .; the second in pentameters, having to do with instruction; the third in hexameters, having to do with contemplation."

[28] (London, 1962), p. 49; American edition, Chicago, 1950.

[29] *Ideas Into Action,* p. 103.

[30] *Barb of Time* (N. Y., 1969). He is led to such distorted statements as "The Renaissance, for Pound, is generally a time of violent disorder and decay in the spheres of religion, morality, politics, and art" (p. 53), a statement disproved by Pound's love of Renaissance art, as in Cantos 9, 26, 45; the statement does have truth with respect to literature *(Spirit,* pp. 216 ff.)

[31] As in *Letters,* p. 331; *Paris Review, 28,* 47.

[32] Davenport, *Motive and Method,* ed. Leary, pp. 52 ff.

[33] Succinct study of their relationship by Richard Ellmann, "Ez and Old Billyum," *New Approaches,* ed. Hesse, pp. 55 ff.

[34] *Idea of a Theater* (rpt. N. Y., 1954), pp. 17 ff.; *Dante's Drama of the Mind* (rpt. Princeton, 1968).

[35] Forrest Read, *New Approaches,* ed. Hesse, pp. 134 ff.

NOTES TO CHAPTER 4

[1] Reprinted with permission of E. P. Dutton from *Medieval Song,* ed. Wilhelm, p. 228. Text: *Lyric Poetry,* ed. Foster and Boyde, *1,* 30. Dante wrote a sirventès on the ladies of Florence *(V. N.* VI), and Beatrice was named ninth, not thirtieth.

[2] *Essays*, pp. 173, 176, 180. See Luigi Valli, *Il Linguaggio segreto di Dante* (Rome, 1928).

[3] Pp. 20 f. (essay dated 1910); cf. Mario Casella, "Cavalcanti, Guido," *Enciclopedia Italiana* (1931), who prefers birth date toward 1255; Villani, *Cronica* VII.15, VIII. 42; Compagni, *Cronica*, I.20.

[4] See *Inf.*, ed. C. S. Singleton, *2*, 148: Farinata died in 1264; the marriage was arranged c. 1267; thus the two men are not necessarily close. See Barbi, "Il Canto di Farinata," *SD, 8* (1924), 87 ff.

[5] For Dante's disapproving views, see *Conv.* IV.vi.12, II.viii.13.

[6] *Mimesis*, tr. W. R. Trask (rpt. Princeton, 1968), pp. 174 ff.

[7] *Il Sonetto a Dante di G. C.* (Turin, 1962), esp. 39 ff.; cf. D'Ovidio, *Studi sulla "D. C.," 1*, 320 ff.

[8] Contini, *Poeti del Duecento, 2, 403* ff.

[9] "Isolated Superiority," *Dial, 84* (1928), 4-7.

[10] As, for example, in the unpublished letter in the Cornell University Library written to Wyndham Lewis, posted Oct. 9, 1956: "Shd/ we add that the Possum went and died there??" [in England].

[11] Kenner, *Pound Era*, p. 553.

[12] *Dictionary of Proper Names* (Oxford, 1898), p. 531.

[13] *Mediaeval Mind*, 4th ed. 2 vols. (Cambridge, Mass., 1951), *2,* 577. Cf. T. K. Swing, *Fragile Leaves of the Sibyl* (Westminster, Md., 1962).

[14] Mazzeo: *Medieval Cultural Tradition in Dante's "Comedy"* (Ithaca, 1960), esp. pp. 101 ff., and *Structure and Thought in "Paradiso"* (Ithaca, 1958), esp. pp. 111 ff.; Chioccioni: *L'Agostinismo nella "D. C."* (Florence, 1952). Also, the Poundlike light analysis in Egidio Guidubaldi, *Dante europeo, 2* vols. (Florence, 1965-66): *2, Il Paradiso come universo di luce.*

[15] *Studi di filosofia medievale* (Rome, 1960), pp. 46 ff. For Arabic tendencies, see Miguel Asín Palacios, *La Escatologìa musulmana en la "D. C."* (Madrid, 1919); Enrico Cerulli, *Il "Libro della scala" e la questione delle fonti arabo-spagnole della "D. C."* (Vatican City, 1949).

[16] *Interpretations of Poetry and Religion* (N.Y., 1900), p. 120.

NOTES TO CHAPTER 5

[1] *Sonnets and Ballate of G. C.* (see Bibl.); *Guido Cavalcanti: Rime; Make It New*, pp. 345 ff.; *Tre Canzoni di G. C.*, introd. Olga Rudge, Quaderni dell'Accademia Musicale Chigiana, 19 (1949); *E. P.'s Cavalcanti Poems;* a series of essays in *Dial, 84* (1928), 231-37, and *85* (1928), 1-20, and *86* (1929), 559-68.

[2] *Letters*, pp. 88, 109, 181, 218, 304 f., etc.

[3] *E. P.'s Cavalcanti Poems*, p. 7.

[4] *Rime di G. C.* . . . . with *Commento di Dino del Garbo*, ed. Antonio Cicciaporci (Florence, 1813), pp. 60 ff., 63, etc.

[5] *Rime,* ed. Cattaneo (Turin, 1967), based on ed. of Guido Favati (Milan, 1957).

[6] *Essays,* pp. 180-82; p. 182: "The 'tondo sesto' may be the 'tondo di Sesto' ('Empirico')." Cf. Cattaneo, who follows Ercole in arguing for a quarter of Florence (p. 69, n. 6).

[7] For a critical assessment, see Anne Paolucci, "E. P. and D. G. Rossetti as Translators of G. C.," *RR, 51* (1960), 256-67.

[8] *A Portrait of the Artist as a Young Man* in *Viking Portable James Joyce,* ed. Harry Levin (New York, 1947), p. 436.

[9] Ed. Otto Bird, *MS 2* (1940), 150-203, and *3* (1941), 117-60.

[10] *Espositione . . . sopra la Canzone d'Amore di G. C. Fiorentino* (Siena, 1602). See *Essays,* p. 160.

[11] *Comento sopra la Canzone di G. C.* (Florence, 1568).

[12] Salvadori, *La Poesia giovanile e la Canzone d'amore di G. C.* (Rome, 1895); Vossler, *Die philosophischen Grundlagen zum 'süssen neuen Stil'* (Heidelberg, 1904).

[13] *Saggi di filosofia dantesca,* 2d ed. (Florence, 1967); *Dante e la cultura medievale,* 2d ed. (Bari, 1949); articles in *SD, 25* (1940), 43-79, and *CN, 6-7* (1946-47), 123-35.

[14] *G. C.'s Theory of Love* (Toronto, 1949).

[15] Shaw, p. 212; Bird, p. 154; see *Letters,* p. 304.

[16] *G. C.'s Theory of Love,* pp. 18 ff. See Albertus Magnus, *Opera omnia, 7,* pt. 1: *De anima,* ed. Clemens Stroick (Munster, 1968), III.1.ix (p. 176): "*sunt quinque sensus interiores, sensus communis, imaginatio, aestimativa, phantasia, et memoria.*" For one of best explanations of pre-Scholastic and Scholastic divisions of the mind, see Etienne Gilson, *AHDLMA, 4* (1929-30), 142-58.

[17] *G. C.'s Theory of Love,* p. 22.

[18] *SD, 25* (1940), 56.

[19] *Essays,* p. 184; cf. Del Garbo, ed. Cicciaporci, p. 83.

[20] II.3.viii (ed. Stroick, p. 110).

[21] *De anima* III.2.xviii (ed. Stroick, p. 205).

[22] *CN, 6-7* (1946-47), 132 f.

[23] *Essays,* pp. 173 f.; see Albertus Magnus, *De anima* I.1.v (ed. Stroick, p. 11); also Canto 63/353:371.

[24] The full line in Cattaneo is *For d'ogne fraude–dico, degno in fede* (Outside all fraud, I say, worthy of faith), but the *dico* is read *dice* by Casella and Shaw (p. 88), with the sense "says one who is worthy of faith" (that is, Guido's source). Shaw shied away from naming anyone (indeed, Albertus would be absurd under the circumstances); Pound read *dice,* but transferred the phrase to Love.

NOTES TO CHAPTER 6

[1] *Vita di Dante* XXVI, ed. Muscetta, p. 50.

[2] Best studies: Gilson, *Dante the Philosopher,* pp. 162 ff.; Nardi, *SD, 25* (1940), 5 ff.

³ The age-old argument in I.v and elsewhere of parts implying a whole might better be interpreted as an argument for democracy, where the will of the Many expresses itself in the voice of the One. See *Kulchur*, pp. 77 f.

⁴ *History of Italian Lit.*, *1*, 148; *Mediaeval Culture*, *1*, 261 ff.

⁵ See *Jefferson and/or Mussolini*, p. 17: "The whole of the *Divina Commedia* is a study of the 'directio voluntatis' (direction of the will)." Also, *Impact*, pp. 122 ff., for a correlation with Mencius.

⁶ *Impact*, p. 66.

⁷ *Essays*, pp. 201 ff., esp. pp. 211 ff.; *Kulchur*, p. 292. See Earle Davis, *Vision Fugitive* (Lawrence, Kans., 1968).

⁸ *Science of Money*, 2d ed. rev. (N. Y., 1896; rpt. N. Y., 1968), pp. 15, 79 ff., etc.; cf. *Kulchur*, p. 185.

⁹ *Make It New*, p. 19. Also in *Impact*, p. 142; *ABC of Reading*, p. 46; first occurrence: *Letters*, p. 247.

¹⁰ Stock, *Life*, pp. 221 ff. For an account, see *To-morrow's Money*, ed. Montgomery Butchart (London, 1936), pp. 155 ff.; also Canto 38, p. 190.

¹¹ Described in *To-morrow's Money*, pp. 13 ff. See Silvio Gesell, *Natural Economic Order*, tr. Philip Pye, rev. ed. (London, 1958; 1st German ed., 1906-11). Pound's ideas contained in *ABC of Economics*.

¹² Introd. Charles Beard (rpt. N. Y., 1943). On the discovery of Adams, see Stock. pp. 380 ff.

¹³ P. 101. See the general critique of Arthur F. Beringause, *Brooks Adams* (N. Y., 1955), pp. 122 ff.

¹⁴ *Science of Money*, p. 1.

¹⁵ *Barbara Villiers: or, A History of Monetary Crimes* (N. Y., 1899), pp. 7 ff.; cf. *History of Monetary Systems* (London, 1895; rpt. N. Y., 1969), pp. 107 ff.

¹⁶ *Usury and the Jews* (San Francisco, 1879), an early work; on the Rothschilds, *Barbara Villiers*, pp. 60 ff.

¹⁷ *Money and Civilization* (1st ed., 1867; rpt. N. Y., 1969), pp. 49 ff.

¹⁸ Unpublished letter to Wyndham Lewis in Cornell University Library, no date, numbered IV 4.

SELECT BIBLIOGRAPHY

I. WORKS OF DANTE IN EDITIONS REFERRED TO IN TEXT

Convivio, edd. G. Busnelli and G. Vandelli, introd. M. Barbi, 2d ed. A. E. Quaglio, 2 vols. Florence: Le Monnier, 1964-68.

De monarchia, ed. P. G. Ricci, Società Dantesca National Edition, Milan: Mondadori, 1965.

De vulgari eloquentia, ed. A. Marigo, 3d ed. P. G. Ricci, Florence: Le Monnier, 1968.

Divina Commedia, ed. G. Petrocchi, Società Dantesca National Edition, 4 vols. Milan: Mondadori: *1. Introduzione*, 1966; *2. Inferno*, 1966; *3. Purgatorio*, 1967; *4. Paradiso*, 1967.

Epistolae: Letters of Dante, ed. P. Toynbee, 2d ed. C. G. Hardie, Oxford: Clarendon, 1966.

Lyric Poetry, ed. K. Foster and P. Boyde, 2 vols. Oxford: Clarendon, 1967.

Vita Nuova, ed. N. Sapegno, 2d ed. Milan: Mursia, 1968.

II. WORKS OF POUND IN EDITIONS REFERRED TO IN TEXT

ABC of Economics, London: Faber, 1933.

ABC of Reading, N. Y.: New Directions Paper, 1971.

A Lume Spento and Other Early Poems, N. Y.: New Directions, 1965.

Cantos, N. Y.: New Directions, 1970; London: Faber, 1968.

Cavalcanti Poems, Verona: New Directions, 1966.

Cavalcanti: Rime, Genoa; Marsano, 1931.

Confucius: Great Digest, Unwobbling Pivot, Analects, N. Y.: New Directions Paper, 1969.

Gaudier-Brzeska: Memoir, London: John Lane, 1916.

Guide to Kulchur, N. Y.: New Directions Paper, 1970 (cited as *Kulchur*).

Impact: Essays on Ignorance and the Decline of American Civilization, ed. N. Stock, Chicago: Regnery, 1960.

Jefferson and/or Mussolini, N. Y.: Liveright Paper, 1970.

Letters, ed. D. D. Paige, N. Y.: Harcourt, Brace, 1950; rpt. *Selected Letters (1907-41)*, New Directions Paper, 1971.

Literary Essays, ed. T. S. Eliot, N. Y.: New Directions Paper, 1972 (cited as *Essays*).

Lustra, N. Y.: Knopf, 1917.

Make It New, New Haven: Yale, 1935.

Pavannes and Divagations, N. Y.: New Directions, 1958.

Personae: Collected Poems, rev. ed. N. Y.: New Directions, 1971.

Pound/Joyce: Letters, ed. F. Read, N. Y.: New Directions Paper, 1967.

Selected Poems, N. Y.: New Directions Paper, 1957.

Selected Prose 1909-1965, N. Y.: New Directions, 1973.

Sonnets and Ballate of Guido Cavalcanti, London: Swift, 1912.

Spirit of Romance, N. Y.: New Directions Paper, 1968 (cited as *Spirit*).

Translations, introd. H. Kenner, 2d ed., N. Y.: New Directions Paper, 1963.

172 *Dante and Pound*

III. BOOKS RELATED TO DANTE

Auerbach, Erich, *Dante: Poet of Secular World,* tr. R. Manheim, Chicago, 1961.
Barbi, Michele, *Life of Dante,* tr. P. G. Ruggiers, Berkeley, 1954.
——*Problemi fondamentali per un nuovo commento della "D. C.,"* Florence, 1955.
Bergin, T. G., *Dante,* N. Y., 1965.
——*Diversity of Dante,* New Brunswick, 1969.
——ed., *From Time to Eternity,* New Haven, 1967.
——*Perspectives on "D. C.,"* New Brunswick, 1967.
Boccaccio, Giovanni, *Vita di Dante,* ed. C. Muscetta, Rome, 1963.
Brandeis, Irma, *Ladder of Vision,* London, 1960.
Cambon, Glauco, *Dante's Craft,* Minneapolis, 1969.
Cavalcanti, Guido, *Rime,* ed. G. Cattaneo, Turin, 1967.
——ed. A. Cicciaporci, Florence, 1813.
——ed. G. Favati, Millan, 1957. (See also listings under Pound)
Chimenz, Siro, *Dante,* Milan, n.d.
Chioccioni, P. Pietro, *L'Agostinismo nella "D. C.,"* Florence, 1952.
Chubb, T. C., *Dante and His World,* Boston, 1966.
Clements, Robert J., *American Critical Essays on "D. C.,"* N. Y., 1967.
Compagni, Dino, *Cronica,* ed. G. Luzzatto, Turin, 1968.
Contini, Gianfranco, *Poeti del Duecento,* 2 vols. Milan, 1960.
Cosmo, Umberto, *Handbook to Dante Studies,* tr. D. Moore, Oxford, 1950.
Croce, Benedetto, *Poesia di Dante,* Bari, 1921; Eng. tr., N. Y., 1922; rpt, 1971.
Curtius, E. R., *European Literature and the Latin Middle Ages,* tr. W. R. Trask, N. Y., 1953.
Davis, C. T., *Dante and the Idea of Rome,* Oxford, 1957.
De Robertis, Domenico, *Il Libro della "Vita Nuova,"* 2d ed., Florence, 1970.
De Sanctis, Francesco, *History of Italian Literature,* tr. J. Redfern, 2 vols. rpt. N. Y., 1968.
D'Ovidio, Francesco, *Studi sulla "D. C.,"* 2 vols., Caserta, 1931.
Dunbar, Helen, *Symbolism in Medieval Thought . . . ,* rpt. N. Y., 1961.
Eliot, T. S., *Selected Essays,* 2d ed. N. Y., 1950.
Fergusson, Francis, *Dante,* N. Y., 1966.
——*Dante's Drama of the Mind,* rpt. Princeton, 1968.
Freccero, John, ed., *Dante,* Englewood Cliffs, N. J., 1965.
Friedrich, Hugo, *Epochen der italienischen Lyrik,* Frankfurt, 1964.
Gardner, E. G., *Dante and the Mystics,* N. Y., rpt. 1968.
Getto, Giovanni, *Letture scelte sulla "D. C."* Florence, 1970.
Gilbert, Allan H., *Dante and His "Comedy,"* N. Y., 1963.
Gilson, Etienne, *Dante the Philosopher,* tr. D. Moore, London, 1948.
Grandgent, C. H., *Dante Alighieri,* N. Y., rpt. 1966.
Guidubaldi, Egidio, *Dante europeo,* 2 vols. Florence, 1965-66.
Hollander, Robert, *Allegory in Dante's "Commedia,"* Princeton, 1969.
Limentani, U., *Mind of Dante,* Cambridge, Eng., 1965.
Mazzeo, Joseph A., *Medieval Cultural Tradition in Dante's "Comedy,"* Ithaca, 1960.
——*Structure and Thought in "Paradiso,"* Ithaca, 1958.
Moore, Edward, *Studies in Dante,* Four Series, Oxford, 1896-1917.

Musa, Mark, ed., *Essays on Dante,* Bloomington, 1964.
Nardi, Bruno, *Dante e la cultura medievale,* 2d ed. Bari, 1949.
————*Saggi di filosofia dantesca,* 2d ed. Florence, 1967.
————*Studi di filosofia medievale,* Rome, 1960.
Panvini, Bruno, *Rime della scuola siciliana,* 2 vols. Florence, 1962-64.
Parodi, E. G., *Poesia e storia nella "D. C.,"* Naples, 1920.
Rossi, Vittorio, *Saggi e discorsi su Dante,* Florence, 1930.
Santangelo, Salvatore, *Dante e i trovatori provenzali,* Catania, 1921.
Santayana, George, *Interpretations of Poetry and Religion,* N. Y., 1900.
————*Three Philosophical Poets: Lucretius, Dante, and Goethe,* Cambridge, Mass., 1927.
Sapegno, Natalino, and Emilio Cecchi, *Storia della letteratura italiana: I, Le Origini e il Duecento,* Milan, 1965.
Scartazzini, G. A., *Companion to Dante,* tr. A. J. Butler, London, 1893.
Shaw, J. E., *Essays on the "Vita Nuova,"* Princeton, 1929.
————*Guido Cavalcanti's Theory of Love,* Toronto, 1949.
Singleton, Charles S., *Dante Studies,* 2 vols. Cambridge, Mass., 1954-58.
————*D. C.: Inferno,* 2 vols. Princeton, 1970; *Purg.,* 2 vols., 1973.
————*Essay on the "Vita Nuova,"* Cambridge, Mass., 1949.
Spoerri, Theophil, *Dante und die europäische Literatur,* Stuttgart, 1963.
Swing, T. K., *Fragile Leaves of the Sibyl,* Westminster, Md., 1962.
Taylor, Henry Osborn, *Medieval Mind,* 4th ed. 2 vols., Cambridge, Mass., 1951.
Toynbee, Paget, *Dante Studies,* Oxford, 1921.
————*Dictionary of Proper Names and Notable Matters in the Works of Dante,* Oxford, 1898; rev. ed. C. S. Singleton, Oxford, 1968.
Valency, Maurice, *In Praise of Love,* N. Y., 1958.
Villani, Giovanni, *Cronica,* ed. F. G. Dragomanni, 4 vols. rpt. Frankfurt, 1969.
Vossler, Karl, *Die philosophischen Grundlagen zum "süssen neuen stil,"* Heidelberg, 1904.
————*Mediaeval Culture,* tr. W. C. Lawton, 2 vols. rpt. N. Y., 1958.
Whitfield, J. H., *Dante and Vergil,* Oxford, 1949.
Wilhelm, James J., *Medieval Song,* N. Y., 1971.
————*Seven Troubadours,* University Park, Pa., 1970.
Williams, Charles, *Figure of Beatrice,* London, 1958.
Zingarelli, Nicola, *Dante,* Milan, 1909.
————*La Vita, i tempi e le opere di Dante,* 3d ed. Milan, 1931.

IV. BOOKS RELATED TO POUND

Annotated Index to the "Cantos" of E. P., edd. J. H. Edwards and W. W. Vasse, rev. ed. Berkeley, 1971.
Baumann, Walter, *Rose in the Steel Dust,* Coral Gables, Fla., 1970.
Brooke-Rose, Christine, *ZBC of E. P.,* Berkeley, 1971.
Cornell, Julien, *Trial of E. P.,* N. Y., 1966.
Davie, Donald, *E. P.: Poet as Sculptor,* N. Y., rpt. 1968.

Davis, Earle, *Vision Fugitive: E. P. and Economics*, Lawrence, Kans., 1968.

Dekker, George, *Sailing After Knowledge*, London, 1963.

De Nagy, N. Christoph, *E. P.'s Poetics and Literary Tradition*, Bern, 1966.

———*Poetry of E. P.: Pre-Imagist Stage*, Bern, 1960.

De Rachewiltz, Mary, *Discretions*, Boston, 1971.

Emery, Clark, *Ideas Into Action*, Coral Gables, Fla., 1958.

Espey, John J., *E. P.'s "Mauberley,"* Berkeley, 1955.

Gallup, Donald, *Bibliography of E. P.*, 2d ed. London, 1969.

Giovannini, Giovanni, *E. P. and Dante*, Utrecht, 1961.

Hall, Donald, "E. P.: Interview," *Paris Review, 28* (1962), 22-51; rpt. *Writers at Work*, 2d Series, introd. V. W. Brooks, N. Y., 1963, pp. 35 ff.

Hesse, Eva, ed., *New Approaches to E. P.*, Berkeley, 1969.

Hutchins, Patricia, *E. P.'s Kensington*, London, 1965.

Jackson, Thomas H., *Early Poetry of E. P.*, Cambridge, Mass., 1968.

Kenner, Hugh, *Poetry of E. P.*, Norfolk, Conn., 1951.

———*Pound Era*, Berkeley, 1971.

Leary, Lewis, ed., *Motive and Method in "Cantos" of E. P.*, N. Y., 1954.

McDougal, Stuart Y., *E. P. and Troubadour Tradition*, Princeton, 1972.

Norman, Charles, *E. P.*, rev. ed. N. Y., 1969.

Pearlman, Daniel D., *Barb of Time*, N. Y., 1969.

Reck, Michael, *E. P.: Close-Up*, N. Y., 1967.

Ruthven, K. K., *Guide to E. P.'s "Personae" (1926)*, Berkeley, 1969.

Schneidau, Herbert N., *E. P.: Image and the Real*, Baton Rouge, 1969.

Stock, Noel, *Life of E. P.*, N. Y., 1970.

Sullivan, J. P., *E. P.: Critical Anthology*, Baltimore, 1970.

Witemeyer, Hugh, *Poetry of E. P.: Forms and Renewal 1908-1920*, Berkeley, 1969.

Yeats, W. B., *Packet for E. P.*, Dublin, 1929; rpt. in *A Vision*, rev. ed. N. Y., 1962.

175

INDEX OF NAMES AND IDEAS

(All persons alphabetized under family or place names: e.g., Alighieri, Dante; Aquitaine, Eleanor of; Aquinas, Thomas; unless a single name is more common: Sordello, Francesca, Ugolino)

ABC of Economics, 92; 170 n.
ABC of Reading, 32 f., 35, 38; 164 f., 170 nn.
Academe, Grove of, 89
accidente, 76
Acheron, 96
Actaeon, 102
Adamo, Master, 108
Adams, Brooks, 37, 91, 93; 170 n.
Adams, John, 78, 81 f., 89, 101, 115 f., 158
Adams Cantos, 107, 122-24, 139
Adams family, 11, 157
Adige, 73
Aeneid, 1, 48 f., 96
Agassiz, Louis, 52, 57 f., 150; 166 n.
Agent Intellect, 77, 83 f.
Agricola, Rudolph, 156
Aguglione, Baldo d', Reform of, 8
Aiken, Conrad, 21
alba, 38 f.
Alberigo, Fra, 99
Albertus Magnus, 76, 78, 80, 82, 85; 169 n.
Albigensians, 72
Aldighiero family, 2
Aldington, Richard, 14
Alexander the Great, 90
Alighieri, Dante: LIFE: 2-10; birth, 2; friends, 3; dating of works, 7 f.; education, 3, 27-33; marriage and children, 3; politics, 4-10, 87-91; compared to Pound, 23-25; INFLUENCES: Cavalcanti, 59-68; classics, Greco-Roman, 27-29; Guinizelli, 35; troubadours, 29-33, 36; Vergil, 27 f., 45; CONCEPTS: of epic, 40, 43-49, 95; of Heaven, 135 f.; of Hell, 95-101; of Purgatory, 115 f.; of rhetoric, 27-35; SUMMARIES: compared with Pound on general technique, 95 f., 113; final evaluation, 156-59; influence on Pound, 156
Alighieri family: Alighiero, 2 f.; Antonia, 3; Beatrice, Sister, 3; Cacciaguida, 2, 6 f., 10, 38, 143; Eliseo, 2; Francesco, 2; Gabriella, 2; Giovanni, 3; Jacopo, 3; Moronto, 2; Pietro, 3
allegory, 33, 44, 59, 62, 99, 124 f., 158

A Lume Spento, 13, 91, 38-41
Anagni, 5
Analects of Confucius, translated, 22
Anderson, Margaret, 15
angels, 76, 97 f., 111
Angiolieri, Cecco, 4
Anjou, Charles of. *See* Charles I
Antef, 147
Antheil, George, 12
antisemitism, 93, 157
Aphrodite, 47
Apollonius of Tyana, 137 f., 140, 153
Apothecaries and Physicians, Guild of, 4
Aquinas, Thomas, 33, 48 f., 51 f., 66, 85, 98, 140, 144; 166 n.
Aquitaine, Eleanor of, 102, 105 f., 110, 118, 131
Aquitaine, William IX, Duke of, 72
Arabic philosophy, 75 f., 83 f.; 168 n.
Arachne, 120
Arbia, 128
Arezzo, Guittone d', 15, 30-32, 59; 165 n.
Argenti, Filippo, 123
aristocracy, 4, 63, 99 f., 127-29
Aristotle: as source for epic form, 45, 48, 58; effect on Cavalcanti, 69, 75, 77 f., 83-85; evil defined, 88 f., 94, 98, 112; influence on *Convivio* and Later Cantos, 138, 140, 143-45, 148, 157 f.; 166 n.
Arles, 36
Armenonville, 126
Arno, 73
Arnold, Benedict, 123
Arnone, Nicola, 73, 75
Arthurian romances, 49, 99
atheism, 61, 84
Athelstan, 94
Auden, W. H., 22
Auerbach, Erich, xi, 29, 36 f., 63, 155; 165-66 nn.
Augustine, 48, 66, 77, 83, 109; 166 n.
authority, divine, 76
avarice, 98
Avars, 140 f.
Averroes, 76, 84
Avicenna, 83
Avignon, 9

Babylonian Captivity of Church, 9, 89
Bacchus, 102
Bach, J. S., 52 f.
Bacon, Baldy, 107
Bancroft, Edward, 123
Bankhead, J. H., 19

178

Douglas, Major C. H., 14, 16, 19, 91
Drummond, John, 3, 55
Dutch East Indies Co., 93

Eagle of Jupiter, 120
Early Cantos: analyzed, 101-13; compared to Dante, 102, 109-13; compared to *Pisan Cantos,* 124, 133 f.; movement in, 101 f.; general, 25, 55
Ecbatan(a), 56, 103
Eclogues (Dante), 10
Eclogues (Vergil), 7, 28
economic ideas: to Dante, 87-91; to Pound, 14, 18 f., 91-94, 119, 129 f., 158
Eden, Garden of, 89
Egoist Magazine, 15
Egyptian religion, 71
Eliot, T. S.: in Pound's life, 14-17, 21 f., 24; literary relationship with Pound, 31, 58; rivalry with, 64 f., 68; general, 83, 119, 126, 137, 164 n., 168 n.
Elissa, 61 f.
Ellmann, Richard, 167 n.
Emery, Clark, x, 55; 165 n., 167 n.
empiricism, 73 f., 76, 85, 98, 112, 147, 150
Empirico. *See* Sesto Empirico
Empyrean, 104
England: as home for Pound, 13-17, 22, 25; in *Cantos,* 116, 130 f.
English charters, 37
English Review, 14
Enna, Vale of, 79
envy, 98
epic, allegorical, 99
epic, traditional, 1, 3, 25, 58, 90, 158
epic of judgement: defined, 1, 23 f., 40 f., 90; meaning to Dante, 43-49; to Pound, 49-58; problems, 90, 158, 167 n.
epicureanism, 62-64
Epicurus, 62
epistemology, medieval, 45, 48, 50, 54 f., 107 f.
Epistles (Dante), 7-10
Erebus, 139
Erigena. *See* Scotus Erigena
Eschenbach, Wolfram von, 90
Este, Parisina d', 110
Este family, 53 f.
Europe, united, 89
evil, concepts of, 97 f., 111 f.
exile: Dante's, 5-10, 24; Pound's, 12 f., 24
eye imagery, 106, 139, 143, 149 f.

Faggiuola, Uguccione della, 9
faith, defined, 152 f.
Farinata. *See* Uberti, F. degli
fascism, 8, 87, 91-94, 158. *See also* Mussolini

fate, 133
Favati, Guido, 70, 80
Fergusson, Francis, xi, 58, 143; 167 n.
Ferrara, 2, 40, 53 f., 113
Fitzgerald, Desmond, 128 f.
Flaubert, Gustave, 31, 34, 58, 105
Fletcher, John Gould, 14 f.
Flint, F. S., 15
Flora, 79
Florence, 2-10, 24, 59, 61, 73
Folquet (of Marseille; Bishop of Toulouse), 135, 142 f.
Ford, Ford Madox, 14
Forlì, 7
Fortune: in Dante, 131 f.; in Pound, 131-33, 148
four (number), 56 f.
Francesca (of Rimini), 90 f., 95, 99, 104 f., 113
Francis of Assisi, 144
fraud, 90, 98, 120
Frederick II, Emperor, 4, 13, 76, 90
Freiburg, 110, 119
French Revolution, 116
Freud, Sigmund, 52, 156
Frobenius, Leo, 37, 52, 126
Frontinus, 32
Frost, Robert, 14, 22, 32
fugue structure, 53, 56
Furies, 62
Fussell, Edwin, x

Gais, 17, 20
Galicia, 61, 70, 72
Galla Placidia, 10, 72
Gallup, Donald, ix, x
Garbo, Dino del, 75 f.; 168-69 nn.
gargoyles, 99, 121
Gaudier-Brzeska, Henri, 15 f., 110
Gemini, 2
Genoa, 20
Gepids, 140 f.
Germany: in Italian politics, 4 f., 8-10; to Dante, 25, 87-91; to Pound, 20, 88
Geryon, 93, 111, 120-22
Gesell, Silvio, 19, 91; 170 n.
Ghibellines, 4-10, 63
Gianni, Lapo, 4, 30, 59 f.
Gilson, Etienne, 66; 169 n.
Giotto, 68
Giovanna, Lady, 59 f., 79
Giovannini, Giovanni, x; 165 n., 167 n.
Giunta, Bernardo da, 75
gluttony, 30, 90, 97
God, proofs of, 88
gold, 90, 92, 140
Goliath, 8
Gothic art, 141
Gourdon, 103

180

justice, 131, 139, 142, 144, 146, 148
Justinian, emperor, 94, 135, 137

Kaltenborn, H. V., 19
K'ang Hsi, 138, 141 f.
Kati (Khaty), 145, 149
Kenner, Hugh, x, 119, 150; 165 n., 168 n.
Khayyam, Omar, 17; 163 n.
Kruif, Paul de, 19
Kuanon (Kuan Yin), 139
Kulchur, Guide to, 37, 51, 54, 88, 91, 93; 164 n., 166 n., 170 n.
Kung. *See* Confucius

Lagia, Lady, 60
lament *(planh)*, 130 f.
lamias, 71, 73
Landor, W. S., 13
Later Cantos: analyzed, 135-53; based on *Convivio*, 143-49; compared with *Paradiso*, 135-43, 147-53; problem of form, 137-42; general, 25, 55, 95 f.
Latini, Brunetto, 3, 61, 97
Latin language, 59, 142
Laughlin, James, 21
Laurentian Library, 75
Lawes, Henry, 12
Lawrence, D. H., 14
Lear, King, 133
Leibnitz, G. W., 52, 57 f.
Lentino (Lentini), Giacomo da, 30
Leo VI, the Wise (Byz. emp.), 141
Leo X, Pope, 10
Leopold II, duke (Tuscany), 157
Lethe, 124
Letters (Dante). See *Epistles*
Letters (Pound), 3, 13, 15, 17, 19, 37, 39, 49 f., 53, 55, 58, 64, 110 f.; in notes, 163 f., 166-68
Levy, Emil, 110, 119
Lewis, Wyndham, 15, 55, 58, 110; 168 n., 170 n.
Library of Congress, xi, 20, 22, 137
light imagery, 49, 69, 77 f., 84, 112 f., 122, 136, 141 f., 149-53
Liguria, 5, 17
Limbo, 100
Limone, 143
Lindsay, Vachel, 32
Linnaeus, 57
Lion (ship), 11
Literary Essays, 14, 37, 65, 75, 105; in notes, 164 f., 168-70
Little Review, 15
Livy, 32
Loba, Lady, 102
Locke, John, 82
Logos, 44 f., 48, 97. *See also* reason
Lomax, Bertold, 40, 43

Lombards, 141
Lombardy, 7, 90
London: as Pound's home, 13-17; in Pound's work, 22, 39, 100 f., 131
Lorris, Guillaume de, 99
Louis XVI (France), 116
Love: as Amor, 60, 72, 74, 145, 151; defined by Dante, 143 f.; operation, 147 f.; related to philosophy, 142
Lowell, Amy, 15
Lucan, 28, 32
Lucca, Bonagiunta da, 15, 30, 59
Luce, Clare Booth, 22
LUE (anagram), 120
lust, 2, 47, 70, 90, 108, 119
Lustra, 53; 166 n.
lyric phase: Dante's, 4, 27-36; Pound's, 36-42
lyric poetry, related to epic, 27-29, 39, 58, 70

MacLeish, Archibald, 22; 164 n.
Madonna. *See* Mary, Virgin
Madonna in Ortolo (painting), 73 f.
Maensac, Pieire de, 104
magic, 60, 90, 126, 133, 153
Maiano, Dante of, 4
Malaspina, Moroello, 7
Malatesta, Gianciotto, 104
Malatesta, Isotta, 107
Malatesta, Paolo, 90 f., 95, 99, 113
Malatesta, Sigismundo, 92, 94, 106-08
Malatesta Cantos, 103, 106-08
Malmaison, 126
Mandetta, Lady, 72
Manfred, 4, 13, 106
Marcher family, 17
Marlowe, Christopher, 69
Mars, 78
Mars, Heaven of, 2
martyrdom, 2
Marx, Karl, 91 f.
Mary, Virgin, 2, 73, 103
Matelda, Matilda, 79
Mathews, Elkin, 13
matter *(hyle)*, 45, 48, 54, 97, 104, 111 f.
Mauleon, Savairic, 104
Mayflower (ship), 11
Mazzeo, Joseph A., 67; 168 n.
Medici, Alessandro dei, 104-106
Medici family, 105, 110
meditation, 54, 108, 144, 157
Medusa, 99
melopoeia, 36
memory *(memora)*, 77 f., 83; 169 n.
Mencius, 37, 57, 138 f.; 170 n.
Merano, 17
Mercure de France, 15
Mercury, Heaven of, 147

182

184

185

INDEX OF ALLUSIONS TO DANTE'S "COMEDY"

INDEX OF ALLUSIONS TO POUND'S "CANTOS"

Canto Number   Page Number in Text

1 51, 101
2 102, 103, 116 f.
3 13, 102, 167 n.
4 72 f., 102, 167 n.
5 103
6 117 f.
7 105 f.
8 106-08
9 106-08, 167 n.
10 106-08
11 106-08
12 107 f.
13 55, 107 f., 139
14 55, 101, 108 f.
15 55, 101, 108 f.
16 16, 55, 109
19 110
20 55, 91, 110, 118, 161
21 72, 110
23 111-13
24 113
26 167 n.
27 74
29 111, 117-19, 161
30 104, 110, 124
31 116
32 116
35 52
36 70, 72, 75-85, 115, 117, 166 n.
37 119
38 119 f., 170 n.
39 91, 152
40 166 n.
41 18
45 115, 167 n.
49 120 f.
51 119-21
52 106, 122
53 150
61 82, 142
62 11

63 78, 169 n.
67 81
69 89, 123
71 18
72-73 (missing) 123 f.
74 20, 55, 74, 124-26, 100, 118, 161
75 9, 36
76 3, 13, 20, 78, 118, 132
77 6, 15, 56, 128, 144
78 124, 129
79 127 f.
80 24, 95, 130 f., 161
81 21
82 13
83 16, 23, 118
84 118, 130
85 130, 137, 139, 144, 151
86 132, 137, 139, 148
87 137, 143 f.
88 121, 137-39, 147
89 122, 139, 147, 152
90 139 f., 161
91 71, 117, 133, 151-53
92 71, 118, 128 f., 136, 142 f.
93 18, 79, 81, 136, 142, 145-50, 161
94 57, 140
95 145
96 133, 141, 148
97 118, 120, 121, 133, 138
98 138, 141 f.
99 57, 138, 141 f.
100 136, 151
102 58
104 57
105 130
107 142, 150
109 106
110 95
111 121
112 133
113 57, 137, 143, 166 n.
116 100, 147, 167 n.
117 157, 161